HOURS OF OPENING

Monday, Tuesday,
Thursday and Friday
10 a.m. — 8 p.m.

Wednesday and Saturday
10 a.m. — 5 p.m.

FINES:—Fines for detention
will be charged according to
the bye-laws.

RENEWALS:—Period of loan
may be renewed if the book
is not required by another
borrower.

**BOOKS DAMAGED OR
LOST:**—Readers are required
to take care of books issued
to them. Loss or damage
must be made good and the
value of books lost or
damaged will be charged.

**This book is due for return
on latest date stamped on
card.**

**PLEASE DO NOT REMOVE
CARD**—6d. fine will be
charged if lost.

AG 10241/69

ALL THE PAINTINGS OF
TITIAN

Part 3
VOLUME THIRTY-ONE
in the
Complete Library of World Art

The Complete Library of World Art

ALL THE PAINTINGS

OF **TITIAN**

Part 3 (1546-1576)

Text by FRANCESCO VALCANOVER

Translated from the Italian by
SYLVIA J. TOMALIN

OLDBOURNE
London

© 1965 by Rizzoli Editore, Milan
Published in Great Britain by
Oldbourne Press, 1–5 Portpool Lane,
London E.C.1

Printed and bound in Great Britain by
Jarrold and Sons Ltd, Norwich

CONTENTS

TITIAN

Life and Work 1546–1576

WHEN Titian arrived in Rome in October 1545, he was warmly welcomed not only by Bembo and Cardinal Alessandro Farnese, but also by the Pope himself, who magnanimously gave him an apartment in the Belvedere. With Vasari and Sebastiano del Piombo as guides, and occasionally even with Bembo, Titian visited the ancient monuments of the city, admired the innumerable examples of classic statuary, and remained for a long time looking at Raphael's frescoes in the Vatican *Stanze* and those of Michelangelo in the Sistine Chapel. Nor did he forget his distant friends, answering the letters of his "comrade," and interceding for Sansovino who had been imprisoned after the disastrous collapse of the San Marco Library.

Above all, however, he dedicated himself to his work—to the many portraits and to a few religious pictures as well as to the *Danaë* (plates 4–5) which he had promised Ottavio Farnese, grandson of Paul III and "young man of the world." It was precisely this picture which Michelangelo (after his visit to Titian in his studio, followed by the usual praises which courtesy required) "commended very highly" to Vasari who had accompanied him, "saying that he liked Titian's coloring and his style very much, but that it was such a pity that in Venice they did not learn to draw well from the very beginning, and that those painters did not study better. That is to say (he added) that if this man had been helped by art and by drawing as he had by nature, particularly in imitating living things, no one could have done more or better work." If this was actually Michelangelo's opinion and not Vasari's, it reflects how little Michelangelo understood of Titian's technique and its independence from the ideals of drawing and of chiaroscuro which governed the older artist's own monumental world. Of course Michelangelo would be both astonished and irritated to see how the figure of Danaë, starting out as an exercise in his own manner, is resolved so sensually and illusionistically in a spirit entirely alien to Michelangelo's own.

If the sensuality of the *Danaë* was not particularly appreciated in Roman circles, still less was the lost *Ecce Homo* which Titian painted "to give as a gift to the Pope" and which according to Vasari, "was as though the works of Michelangelo, Raphael, Polidoro and others had made him lose his way, or (there was) some other reason, because it did not seem to the painters that it was a good work, of the same excellence as many of Titian's others, particularly the portraits."

Among the Roman works, the Naples portrait of *Pope Paul III and His Grandsons* (color plate I), "the first historical scene in modern painting" (Ortolani), stands out. The dramatic gathering of the three participants is realized with wonderful simplicity, in flowing fields of reds, whites and dull purples, applied with quick telling brushstrokes so that nothing of the first dazzling intuition of character is lost. The psychology of the three Farnese—a distant reserve in Alessandro, indomitable and suspicious lust for power in Paul III, obsequious adulation in Ottavio (plate 1)—are expressed with such openness that it is not to be wondered at if, as has been supposed, the Pope and his family did not press Titian to finish the work.

8

Equally penetrating studies in character are to be found in the other Farnese portraits now in Naples: the *Cardinal Alessandro* (plate 3) cold and calculating in the same way as he appears behind the Pope in the other picture; *Pope Paul III wearing the Papal Cap* (plate 2), certainly dating from this time because of the Pope's great age in the portrait with his grandsons; and *Pier Luigi Farnese* (plate 7), possibly executed in Piacenza. This harsh tyrant was to be murdered in 1547 in the plot organized by Federico Gonzaga with the connivance of Charles V.

Titian's productive stay in Papal Rome came triumphantly to an end in March 1546 when Roman citizenship was conferred on him in a ceremony at the Capitol. On his return journey, he stopped in Florence to offer his services to Grand Duke Cosimo—without success, however. He then hurried on to Venice, where he had many commitments awaiting him, including the portrait (now lost) of the newly-elected Doge Francesco Donato for the official collection of the Venetian Republic, and the altarpiece for the Cathedral of Serravalle he had started in 1542. He himself did not work particularly hard on the altarpiece (plate 12), and while he retained the composition which is oratorical in style and was conceived before he left for Rome, the actual execution of the picture was left largely to his workshop—as is obvious from its mediocre quality. Few if any pupils, however, had a hand in the San Lio altarpiece (plate 13), in which the complex Mannerist drawing of the Saint's pathetic figure, dominant against the open stormy sky, lacks any abstract value, resolved as it is in the warm grey and golden brown tones which blend superbly with the red cloak.

To this same period belongs one of Titian's major works: the *Votive Portrait of the Vendramin Family* (plate 14) now in London. New and convincing arguments have revised its traditional dating of about 1552. Here the historical and psychological representation brings to mind the portrait of *Pope Paul III and His Grandsons*, and the composition recalls once more the lost *Votive Portrait of the Doge Andrea Gritti* (plate 190). However, since the disturbing contrast of characters we find in the Farnese picture has no place here, since every architectural element (apart from the altar and three steps) has disappeared, and since a religious symbol takes the place of sacred images, there are only the human figures themselves to construct the space by their solemn movements. Against the spacious blue-gray sky, the sumptuous tints with which the figures are painted glow in a wonderfully intense relationship: the greens, grays and reds of the children on the right, the blacks, whites, reds and oranges of those on the left, and the triumphantly dominating range of reds in the ceremonial robes of the adults. Thus the scene, through the splendor of its pictorial material alone, becomes an apotheosis.

Only a year after Titian had taken up his work again in the tranquility of his Birri house, Charles V invited him to come to Augsburg where the Emperor had convoked the Diet of the Empire for the spring of 1548, after the victory of Mühlberg over the Protestant League of Smalcalda. Titian did not want to miss this historic occasion, so, ending his repeated requests to the Papal Court for the "Lead Office" (an honorific concession which had remained empty after the death of Luciani), he started out for Augsburg at the beginning of January 1548 accompanied by his son Orazio, his nephew Cesare, and his Dutch pupil Lambert Sustris. He took with him as gifts for the Emperor an *Ecce Homo* (plate 20), and a *Venus*, now lost.

He found life in the Bavarian city seething with vitality. Gathered there were princes, counts and electors in all the magnificence of the Imperial Court—and all of them leading personalities in the contemporary history of Europe. It was a stimulating occasion for a series of portraits which today, unfortunately, are mostly scattered or destroyed. Among the first to pose was Charles V himself. In the equestrian portrait (plate 22), now in the Prado, the Emperor appears on the battlefield of Mühlberg, sinister in its emptiness. He is sitting erect in his richly decorated armor staring fixedly into space (plate 23). In the heroic immobility of the pose, the figure loses all its humanity and becomes instead a heroic symbol of mythical royal power.

In the second portrait of the Emperor executed in Augsburg in 1548 (plate 21), Titian no longer portrays the idealized sovereign in the hour of victory, but rather the physically weakened human being who is already contemplating giving up the grave responsibilities of power. Against the liveliness of the red carpet, the yellow-orange drapery and the black clothes, the immobility of Charles V's face stands out in startling clarity as he sinks back into the chair. So too in the posthumous Prado *Portrait of Isabella of Portugal* (plate 25), the face of the Empress stands out like marble against the deep violet of the sumptuous brocades, and seems veiled in melancholy, almost as though taking a sad farewell of the world.

We can also date from 1548 the *Portrait of Nicolas Perrenot Granvella* (plate 26) in Besançon, and that of his son *Antonio*, Bishop of Arras (plate 27); also, possibly, the Vienna *Portrait of John Frederick of Saxony* (plate 29), marvelous for the perception with which the obstinate will of the loser of Mühlberg is characterized.

Involved as he was in numerous and difficult portrait commissions, Titian during his first stay in Augsburg was also doing some paintings, both sacred and profane, for Nicolas

Perrenot Granvella. Among these was a *Venus, Cupid and an Organist* which can almost certainly be identified with the Prado painting (plate 32) from which the other versions derive—those in Berlin (plate 34), in the Uffizi (plate 35), and the other in the Prado (plate 33). The same softly luminous atmosphere as in the Naples *Danaë* pervades this painting, but it is renewed by the color which is shot through with the light illuminating the figure of the young organist and the landscape submerged in the glow of the dying day. The execution, however, here and there betrays some help, especially in the curtain and the drapery on which the nude lies.

Laden with honors, Titian left Augsburg in the late summer of 1548, and after a brief stay in Innsbruck to start the portrait of Ferdinand I's daughters (and to set up a money-making venture in the timber trade), reached Venice at the end of October. Here, while his workshop saw to the execution of various pictures for provincial churches (plates 159, 160 and 161a)—sometimes Titian himself took a hand in them too (plate 36)—he began work on commissions received in Augsburg. Among these were the particularly laborious series called "of the Furies" or "of the Condemned" for Marie, the Queen of Hungary and sister of Charles V. In the two surviving canvases of this series in the Prado (plates 30 and 31), a feeling of savage fury is made palpable by the use of paint alone, since the plastic impetuosity of these two gigantic figures, while echoing the athletic Biblical characters on the ceiling of the Salute (Part 2, plates 179, 180 and 181) which in turn recall Michelangelo, is absorbed in the almost monochromatic range of golden browns which are picked out by the dazzling flashes of light.

In the autumn of 1550, Titian had to break off all his undertakings to return to Augsburg where Charles V had gathered together all the most important members of the Imperial family. The artist's main task was to paint the portrait of Prince Philip who, in spite of the opposition of his uncle Ferdinand I and his cousin Maximilian, was by now destined to succeed Charles because he was growing increasingly tired and sick and ready to retire from the pressures of public life. In this portrait (plate 43), now in the Prado, the twenty-four-year-old Prince appears in a standing pose, clothed in tight-fitting armor richly decorated in gold— almost a heraldic figure, with his feathered helmet and steel gloves shining from the shadows where the deep violet of the tablecloth and the outlines of the pedestal shimmer with tenuous flashes of luminosity.

The *Portrait of Philip II* in Cincinnati (plate 42) is without any such symbolic intent. The version in the Rasch Collection (plate 49) is based on this picture, which is possibly identifiable in the "rapid sketch" which Titian started during the Prince's brief stay in Milan at the end of 1548. Other portraits which may be dated 1550 or slightly later possess the same sureness of characterization and just as free a pictorial idiom: for example, the Prado *Supposed Portrait of a Knight of Malta* (plate 45), the San Francisco *Friend of Titian* (plate 46b), and the Melbourne *Franciscan* (plate 47b). It makes little difference that the identity of the sitters is unknown, since they are painted with natural immediacy. Then there are the Lugano *Antonio Anselmi* (plate 39), the *Supposed Portrait of Benedetto Varchi* in Vienna (plate 38), the Uffizi *Ludovico Beccadelli* (plate 47a)—all reposing in an affable reserve which reflects the cultured, sensitive intelligence of the sitters; and the Lugano *Doge Francesco Venier* (plate 50), magically evoked in his ceremonial robes against the somber red of the curtain, while on the left the lagoon is lighted by a blood-red fire. Among the official portraits painted during this period are the Naples *Philip II* (plate 48), in a dignified pose against the uniform gray of the background, and the Kassel *Portrait of a Gentleman* (plate 40), an ostentatious figure in red and yellow portrayed in an arrogant pose against the tremendous landscape—which was possibly added later as its dissolved effect is more characteristic of Titian's later works.

On his return from Augsburg to Venice, where he is recorded as being in August 1551, Titian continually worked to satisfy the ever-increasing requests of the Hapsburg family (particularly Prince Philip, who was shortly to monopolize Titian's production of paintings), but did not neglect his portrait-painting duties for the Venetian Republic, nor did he refuse some important ecclesiastical commissions. With so much work, the painter occasionally betrays moments of fatigue in this period which certainly cannot be attributed to his workshop. Thus, if in the Brera *St Jerome in the Wilderness* (plate 65) and the Escorial *St Margaret and the Dragon* (plate 52), the formal Mannerist touches are added to a dense structural color formed by a light which gives dramatic pathos to figures and landscape alike, in the Medole altarpiece (plate 64), in the Salute *Pentecost* (plate 70), and in the Prado *Holy Trinity* (plate 53) the obvious search for religious and allegorical content blocks the vitality of the color in clear cold areas which accentuate the scenic effects by giving a feeling of other-worldliness to the sacred images, paralleling the contemporary creations of Tintoretto.

In the various "poesies" for Philip, dating from the same period, Titian again trusts to the expressive possibilities of color. Only in subjects where his inventiveness could express itself freely did he find new incentive. His idiom by then had been progressing towards the fusion of figures and surroundings in tonalities effervescent with light. A comparison of the soft plastic fullness of the Naples *Danaë* (plates

4–5) with the dissolved coloring of the Prado *Danaë* (plate 58) shows how far in less than a decade Titian had moved on the path which was to lead him to the fantastic impressionism of his last paintings. Bathed in golden light, the figures of Danaë and the hag seem almost without weight, figures flowering on the surface of the canvas in sumptuous harmonies of browns, reds and somber grays which float against the intense yellow and deep blue of the sky. As in the *Danaë*, repeated several times with the help of his workshop (plates 59 and 60), so in the Prado *Venus and Adonis* (plate 57) and even more so in the London version (plate 56), the episode of the goddess trying to keep back her lover from his appointment with death has this surface quality. The action is flattened in the foreground, in a spatial conception which is no longer the three-dimensional one of the Renaissance.

No less than in the two "poesies" for Philip, in the Washington *Venus at the Mirror* (plate 62), painted about 1553, the open sensuality of the subject is rendered on a plane of the highest poetry by means of free intensity of pictorial technique. And it can be seen how the compositional scheme of the Vienna *Girl in a Fur* (Part 2, plate 140), renewed in more complex figurative rhythms of classical origin, is enriched in this Washington painting by a luminosity which intensifies the expressive values of the color.

The fact that this "color idea" is not completely realized in *The Martyrdom of St Lawrence* in the Church of the Jesuits in Venice (plate 66) can be explained by assuming that the huge altarpiece, placed there between 1557 and 1559, was commissioned from Titian before 1548. It is most probable that its conception—which is so Mannerist in feeling in the articulated complexity of the perspectives and in the echoes of classical motifs (the imposing colonnade and the altar on which the ancient statue stands)—goes back to Titian's brief stay in Venice in 1547. The picture was taken up again in the late 1550's, and Titian's effort to resolve his dilemma between the demands of form and those of color is evident. The illusion of depth created by the diagonal architectural perspectives, and the plasticity of the figures, are both weakened by the unreal light and the somber, ghostly atmosphere, full of unexpected reflections (plates 67–69).

Atypical of Titian's renewed interest in color, on the other hand, are the Ancona *Crucifixion*, painted in 1558, and the *Annunciation* of San Domenico Maggiore in Naples, which may be dated from the late 1550's. In the Ancona altarpiece (plate 74), the last act of the divine drama is evoked from the night shadows by a livid light: Christ, hanging above the other figures, is tragically isolated against the stormy sky pierced with shafts of moonlight. Below are the grieving Virgin, St Dominic desperately clutching the base of the Cross, and St John, who, with arms outstretched, stands horror-struck. The integrity of the forms, so dynamic and rich with chiaroscuro effects in the much earlier prototype of 1537, disintegrates even further in the Naples *Annunciation* (plate 71), where the Virgin and the Angel as well as the natural background are all diluted by the light to the point where they become frail phantoms instead of solid forms.

No less than the Naples *Annunciation*, the Prado *Entombment* and the Escorial *St Jerome* bear witness to how Titian in these years basically renewed, by means of his unequaled "color alchemy," the subjects he had already painted many years before. In the Prado *Entombment* (plate 79), the tumult of the figures which lean to the left over the body of Christ is realized by the rapidity of the brushstrokes. The *St Jerome* (plate 75), on the other hand, keeps a certain plastic consistency despite the staccato of the lightning, the glaring white of the Saint's flesh, his red cloak, the wild vegetation of the cave and the gleaming landscape.

This cosmic vision of nature, in which the human figure is enveloped and almost consumed, seems even more evident in other masterpieces dating from these years. These include the two versions of *Christ in the Garden of Gethsemane* in the Escorial (plate 104a) and in the Prado (plate 104b)—the latter rendered in a web of light and shadow that becomes almost monochromatic; the *Wisdom* in the Sansoviniana Library (plate 80), an octagonal painting of soft tonal mixtures and luminous transparencies (plate 81); and *The Stoning of St Stephen* (plate 83), the formal conception of which is "pre-Rubens" but welded to the gleaming landscape by the dense atmosphere which unifies the whole composition. Also belonging to this period are the Ascoli Piceno *Stigmatization of St Francis* (plate 100) in which the figures are placed at the edges of the picture to leave room for the spacious landscape in the center (how surprisingly modern is the Saint's head, modeled "in daubs" (plate 101), and the tremendous series of mythological fables sent to Philip II between 1559 and 1562: the Edinburgh *Diana and Actaeon* (plate 84) and *Diana and Callisto* (plate 85), the Harewood *Diana and Actaeon* (plate 87), the Boston *Rape of Europa* (plate 88) and the London *Perseus and Andromeda* (plate 89).

By this time, the new feeling for humanity which moves Titian more and more deeply reaches an incomparable degree of imaginative expression. All formal canons of the Renaissance are put aside, while the essence of the world of the spirit is retained. The master's visionary evocation of Christian mysteries and of mythology finds its most immediate and striking expression in his exploitation of color.

The Dresden *Portrait of a Girl* (plate 61) and the Berlin *Girl with Dish of Fruit* (plate 63) are already signs of his exploitation. The two paintings are the first of a series of portraits in which Titian's dialogue with his models becomes much more direct and intense than in most of his earlier portraits. After the Vienna *Fabrizio Salvaresio* (plate 92) which bears the date 1558, come the two male portraits in Baltimore and Dresden, the first (plate 95) in three-quarters profile against a dark background, the second (plate 96) in an almost completely frontal pose. To a later date belong the *Portrait of an Oriental Potentate* (Brass Collection, Venice; plate 106), bathed in a dazzling pictorial richness of greens and grays, and the Detroit *Man with a Flute* (plate 94) which almost recalls Rembrandt in the way the flickering light brings forth from the shadows the face and hands of this mysterious man. With similar transmuting force the light models the physical features of the artist himself in the Berlin *Self-Portrait* (plate 98): against the complex scale of tones and semitones and raking light, Titian's countenance stands out, his lined features still full of energy. As in the *Portrait of Pietro Aretino* (Part 2, plate 193), it seems entirely possible that Titian may have purposely left this painting unfinished, realizing that he had achieved a convincing and faithful mirror of life itself.

In these years of intense activity, it was only natural that Titian should turn with increasing frequency to his workshop, which had, for some time, been highly efficient, in order to get through his numerous commissions. From the studio in Birri Grande more and more canvases poured forth—canvases which were reworkings of pictures started many years earlier, replicas with variations, and copies. They were painted by a large group of pupils under the more or less vigilant eye of the master; and it is not surprising that Titian availed himself of their services not only in minor pictures but also for works of some importance. Among these were the votive picture of *Doge Grimani* in the Ducal Palace (plate 102), started in 1556 and still in an unfinished state when Vasari saw it ten years later; *The Transfiguration* in San Salvatore in Venice (plate 103), now hardly fit to be judged because of the careless restoration; the San Sebastiano altarpiece (plate 107), sketched probably in the 1540's and "painted over" by Titian's helpers for the chapel acquired in 1563 by Nicolò Crasso; and the two versions of *The Adoration of the Magi* in the Escorial (plate 76) and in the Ambrosiana (plate 77). The work of helpers is still more obvious in the grandiloquent Escorial *Last Supper* (plate 105), sent to Spain in 1564 and possibly a replica of the one now lost, formerly in the Church of SS Giovanni and Paolo: this hypothesis is confirmed by the contrast between the intensity of the painting in the landscape and the formal academicism of the composition which echoes Leonardo's *Last Supper*.

If the Escorial *Last Supper* is one of those many paintings in which it is difficult to establish how much Titian did (also because of the inevitable alterations caused by restorers), in the works which he painted alone his presence can be felt in all its unique power. Incontrovertible touchstones from the mid-60's which illustrate this are the Borghese Gallery *Venus Blindfolding Cupid*, the Escorial *Crucifixion*, *The Annunciation* of San Salvatore in Venice, and the Hermitage *St Mary Magdalene*.

In this last painting (plate 112), the admirable orchestration of the landscape is in harmony with the mystical ecstasy, which clashes with the sensuality of the female figure in the earlier prototype in the Pitti (Part 2, plate 138). Titian renews with desperate grandeur the themes of the Ancona *Crucifixion* (plate 74) and the Naples *Annunciation* (plate 71) in the paintings in the Escorial (plate 110) and in San

Salvatore (plate 108). Christ rises above nature which witnesses and reflects the divine drama: the sky is riven with lightning and the landscape darkens under the last glimmers of the sunset, while the tiny figures of the holy women and the soldiers hurry through the dense atmosphere toward the distant city. In the Venetian *Annunciation*, the figures of the Angel and the Virgin dissolve in the iridescent air.

The mythical fable of the Borghese *Venus Blindfolding Cupid* (plate 114) goes back to the happy world of youth. One searches in vain, however, for any Phidian serenity in the urgent rhythms of the tones: "a mixture of brushstrokes laden with color, in turn red, turquoise and black, and here and there even grayish and pale blue" (Cavalcaselle). Here the pagan myth is relived. Nature and idea miraculously fuse. It is evident that Titian was allowing himself for the last time to render a happy humanity and a friendly nature.

From now on, further and further removed from the world, and alone with his fantasies, Titian will withdraw to his memories. So we find him in the small votive altarpiece of Pieve di Cadore (plate 125) and in the Prado *Self-Portrait* (plate 128), where he portrays himself at eighty years of age, a brush in his hand, his face sunken as though he were looking back at the events, both happy and sad, of the last few years: his favorite daughter Lavinia's marriage, his reconciliation with his eldest son Pomponio, the deaths of Pietro Aretino in 1556, of Charles V in 1558, of his brother Francesco in 1559, and of Sansovino in 1570.

Even if he was withdrawn, life often roused him from his dreaming. With dignified and obstinate insistence he reminded Philip II constantly of the large sums of money due to him; when Philip replied merely by requesting more paintings, the artist turned to more modest but also more solvent patrons—even assuming such laborious undertakings as the three lost canvases for the ceiling of the Palazzo Pubblico in Brescia (plate 197), which he had to entrust largely to his helpers (as may be gathered from the resentful grumblings of the city fathers of Brescia), or the frescoes for the parish church in Pieve di Cadore, finished from his cartoons in 1567 by Cesare Vecellio, Emanuele da Augusta and Valerio Zuccato. Just as he did not consider it beneath his dignity to enter the commercial timber trade (among his clients in 1564 was the Duke of Urbino), so he did not let slip the opportunity to make money offered by the monopoly on the prints which Cornelio Cort and Nicolò Baldrini were making from some of his works. Nor did he neglect— always with the help of his devoted son Orazio—his property in Cadore or collecting his Milanese and Neapolitan pensions, the receipts of which he mislaid—"being of great age" as García wrote in 1563 to Philip II.

However, neither these practical matters necessary for running his household, nor the honors heaped on him— among others, the election in 1566 as a Member of the Academy of Tuscan Painters and Sculptors—nor the visits paid him by famous people like Vasari in 1566, and Henry II in 1574—limited Titian's usual painting activities. Indeed, it was just when admirers, patrons and disciples were casting doubt on his physical capacities (as though these could condition his creative vision) that he created another great style, a new adventure in the limits of lyric expression.

No less expressive than Lotto's *Andrea Odoni*, the Vienna *Jacopo Strada* (plate 122) is caught in the gesture of offering to an imaginary enthusiast a little statue of Venus—alluding, as do the other objects on the table, to the Mantuan's profession as antiquarian. The sumptuous tints of dark green, purple and black, against which the intense red of the sleeves stands out, are infused with golden light which wonderfully harmonizes the movements and background details in spite of the instability of the sitter's pose.

Dated 1566 but redone in 1568, the Strada picture is the last documented in Titian's incomparable portrait gallery. The artist was now no longer interested in the characterization of the human figure, but only in its fragile "emergence," suggesting its communion with nature. His last masterpieces, destined mostly for Philip II, were created in this spirit. Some of them were seen by Vasari during his Venetian stay in 1566. Whether they were free replicas of earlier works, or even reworkings of paintings started many years before, the expressive values of this new pictorial idiom gave life to incredible images. Titian's sense of drama and his capacity to depict spiritual tension found greater realization.

Every trace of Mannerism, which still disturbs the stylistic unity of the picture in the Church of the Jesuits (plate 66), has disappeared in the Escorial *Martyrdom of St Lawrence* (plate 121), and the forms dissolving in the reddish light of the flares seem phantoms in the dense night atmosphere. In the Prado *St Margaret* (plate 113), a strip of light reveals the dramatic scene and picks out the shimmering green of her tunic against the glow from the fire. In the Prado *Entombment* (plate 124), the feeling is even deeper than in the earlier version (plate 79), and intensified by means of the impasto and the mysterious "*non finito*."

A similar ethereal form can be found in the allegorical *Spain Coming to the Aid of Religion* in the Prado (plate 130), an adaptation of a mythical fable started for Alfonso d'Este, but which, "because of that gentleman's death . . . was not finished, and remained in Titian's hands" (Vasari). The traditional placing of the figures is radically transformed by the shining tonal array whose evocative power is heightened by a much freer rendering. And in the luminosity of the sunset, the figures of Spain in a rose-colored robe, and Religion draped in blue, seem to melt into the landscape, into the intense azure sea, the pale pink sky, the cinder-gray clouds and the somber brown trees.

The impact of the Prado *Fall of Man* (plate 129) is just as intense. This is another painting probably started many years earlier, in which Adam's bronzed flesh and the dazzling whiteness of Eve's are absorbed into the landscape, its azures, grays, yellows, pinks and greens incandescent in the daylight.

In the Prado painting, commissioned in 1571 to celebrate the victorious Battle of Lepanto (plate 131), the figures of Philip II and the Turk in chains suffer from the allegorical intent and the extensive restoration by Carducho. But marvelous things still remain in it: the flaming Angel and the naval battle taking place in the heavy night atmosphere lit by flashes of broadsides.

Titian continues to paint his final works up to the very last hours of his life, expressing, almost for himself alone, the metaphysical meanings of his "color alchemy."

Profound religious feeling pervades the tragic fervor of the Leningrad *St Sebastian* (plate 132): the hero's agony seems shared by the forces of nature. The agony reappears with greater poignancy in the Munich *Crown of Thorns* (plate 134), where the plastic tension of the forms, so violently forced in the Louvre prototype (Part 2, plate 170), is dissolved in the color. An even more intimate spirituality is evoked by the small altarpiece of Pieve di Cadore (plate 125), already mentioned, and the London *Madonna and Child* (plate 139), a sublime mixture of color highlights in a mother-of-pearl light against a golden gray background.

The savage brutality of the Cambridge *Tarquin and*

Lucretia (plate 136), is dramatically conveyed by the pervading reds; the same savagery is epitomized in the Vienna version (plate 137) which repeats the focal point of the scene. The turbulent arabesques, formed by blobs of color applied with the fingers are concrete and exciting means for evoking the passionate content of the painting. A still more tragic image is the Kromieriz *Punishment of Marsyas* (plate 143), where the cruelty of the myth finds expression in the violence of the color.

In the Rotterdam *Child with Dogs* (plate 140) and the Vienna *Nymph and Shepherd* (plate 141), this tumult of color diminishes, and becomes a last nostalgic farewell to youthful themes, veiled now in quiet sadness. The fantastic breaking-down of forms into pure entities of color and light provides a vivid poetic resolution both to the composition as a whole and to each of its details (plate 142).

Thus the end of a long road is reached. Titian's art, sometimes dramatic, sometimes deeply affected by a nostalgia for lost happiness, is transmuted to profound Christian piety in the Venice *Deposition* (plate 144), the huge canvas which was to decorate the funeral monument the artist wanted for himself in the Chapel of the Crucifix in the Frari church. An inexplicable light hovers over the masonry in the background and reflects from the mosaic-lined apse, while the statues and participants seem equally consumed by grief. Along the diagonal, formed by the human figures, we can see the force of their grief: Mary Magdalene with an irrepressible cry turns off-balance; the Virgin, petrified in anguished contemplation, supports the body of Christ; St Jerome anxiously thrusts forward as if expecting a last word from the Son of Man.

While still intent on this masterpiece, Titian died on August 27, 1576, in his house at Birri Grande, deserted because of the plague which raged throughout the lagoon. Shortly before, Vasari had written: "Titian is in the best of health, and has been most fortunate—more than any of his peers have ever been before him; and he has had nothing from Heaven but good fortune and happiness." It is true that his life proceeded without major difficulties and he lived it with dignity; his art reflects the success he enjoyed. His painting developed with sureness and with a tremendous multiplicity of interests. The crisis which tormented the civil and religious history of the century appears in his work to be dominated by a noble and lofty view of the world which was truly Renaissance in spirit.

BIOGRAPHICAL NOTES

1545. Titian leaves the Court of the Duke of Urbino and comes to Rome in October. Here he is welcomed by Bembo, by Alessandro Cardinal Farnese, and by Pope Paul III himself. Vasari and Sebastiano del Piombo accompany him on his visits to the monuments of the city; he meets Michelangelo. For the Farnese family, he paints a *Mary Magdalene* and an *Ecce Homo*, as well as many portraits; for Ottavio, the Pope's grandson and a "young man of the world," the *Danaë* now in the Naples National Gallery.

1546. On March 19, citizenship is conferred on Titian by the City of Rome in a solemn ceremony. On his journey home to Venice, he stops in Florence and offers his services to the Grand Duke—without success, however. On his arrival in Venice, he paints the portrait of Doge Francesco Donato, successor to Pietro Lando who died on November 8 of the previous year.

1547. He finishes the altarpiece for the Cathedral of Serravalle (*Madonna and Child in Glory, and SS Peter and Paul*) started in 1542. A controversy arises with the Building Office of the church, because the artist changed St Vincent to St Peter; this controversy is not resolved until 1553. Sebastian del Piombo dies. Titian asks Alessandro Farnese insistently for the office that Piombo held, but it is granted to Girolamo della Porta. Charles V invites Titian to Augsburg.

1548. In January, Titian with his son Orazio, his nephew Cesare Vecellio and Lambert Sustris, leave Venice for Augsburg, taking with him an *Ecce Homo*. In the spring, he is present at the pomp and magnificence of the gathering of princes, dukes, counts and electors for the Diet in Augsburg. He paints the portraits of many famous people, including Emperor Charles V, his prisoners John Frederick of Saxony and Filippo d'Assia, Queen Marie of Hungary, King Ferdinand and his sons, Emanuele Filiberto d'Aosta, and the Duke of Alba. On the return journey to Venice, he stays in Innsbruck, where he paints the portraits of the daughters of King Ferdinand I, brother of Charles V. He is in Venice by the end of October and paints the portrait of Prince Philip, son of Charles V, in Milan in December.

1549. The engraving of *The Drowning of Pharaoh,* made by Domenico delle Greche, a Spanish student of Titian's, from a Titian drawing is published. Paul III dies and is succeeded by Julius III. In October, Titian finishes a portrait of Prince Philip for Granvella, Bishop of Arras. He sends a portrait of Charles V to Ferrante Gonzaga in Milan. He is working in the parish church of Castello Roganzuolo on the polyptych which was commissioned in 1543.

1550. Titian is in Augsburg in November for the second time, because Charles V gathered together there, in July, members of the Diet, and his family in November, in preparation for his approaching withdrawal from public life. Titian paints a portrait of Prince Philip, and pleads with the Emperor that his friend Pietro Aretino be made a cardinal.

1551. In August, Titian is back in Venice again.

1552. He tells Prince Philip that he has sent him a *Landscape* and the *Portrait of St Margaret*. The beginning of the correspondence between Titian and Philip which grows with the years: the Prince asking continually for paintings, the artist for their payment. From October 29 onwards, Titian again receives the benefits of the Brokerage Office of the Salt Monopoly.

1553. He is finishing some "poesies" for Prince Philip; he paints the prelate Beccadelli's portrait, and also Marcantonio Trevisan's portrait when he becomes doge on the Doge Donà's death.

1554. On October 11, the canvases of the *Holy Trinity* and a *Mater Dolorosa* are sent to Flanders. In reporting that they have been sent, Titian complains to Charles V that he still has not received the two hundred scudi promised in Milan, or the pension of five hundred scudi for his son. In the autumn, he sends the *Venus and Adonis* to the new King of England (Philip II of Spain, husband of Mary Tudor) and promises the *Perseus and Andromeda, Jason and Medea* and a "most pious work." The Canonry of Medole, taken away from his son Pomponio who was little suited to an ecclesiastical career, is given instead to one of

Titian's nephews. To win the approval of the townspeople for the new canon, Titian gives the altarpiece for the main altar of the Church of Santa Maria (*The Risen Christ Appearing to His Mother*). The Doge Marcantonio Trevisan dies and is succeeded by Francesco Venier, who poses for his own portrait and commissions a votive picture of his predecessor.

1555. He finishes the official portrait of the Doge Francesco Venier: it was the last one Titian painted for the official collection of the Venetian Republic. However, although he did not execute the official portraits of the succeeding doges, he still kept his license for the Brokerage Office. His daughter Lavinia marries Cornelio Sarcinelli di Serravalle, taking with her a dowry of 1400 ducats. Titian is commissioned to paint a votive picture of the Doge Francesco Grimani: during 1556 he works on this painting, which was seen by Vasari in the artist's studio in 1566 still in an unfinished state, and which was probably completed by his pupils after his death. Charles V abdicates, taking the painting of the *Holy Trinity* with him to the solitude of Juste.

1556. Death of Pietro Aretino. Lorenzo Priuli succeeds Francesco Venier as Doge. Titian is a member of the jury to judge the ceiling decoration of the Sansoviniana Library.

1557. He sends his son Orazio to Milan to collect his pension. Reconciliation between Titian and his son Pomponio; Titian obtains for him the living of Sant' Andrea del Fabbio. In November he sends Philip II an *Entombment*—which, however, never reached Madrid because it was lost by the Trent postmaster, Lorenzo Bordogna de Tassis.

1558. Death of Charles V at Juste on September 21. Philip II succeeds him, and orders that Titian be paid the arrears of his various pensions.

1559. Death of Titian's elder brother Francesco. Titian tells Philip II that he has sent him a new *Entombment,* the *Diana and Actaeon,* and the *Diana and Callisto.* At the same time he is finishing the *"Christ in the Garden of Gethsemane* and two other compositions": *The Rape of Europa* and *Actaeon Torn to Pieces by the Dogs.*

1560. In many letters to Philip II, Titian assures him that the *Rape of Europa* and *Christ in the Garden of Gethsemane* are almost finished, and mentions some scenes of *Caesar's Victories.* He is paid the shipping expenses of an *Adoration of the Magi* sent to Spain the year before.

1561. In November, in Venice, he gives Garcia Hernandez (Philip II's secretary) a *Mary Magdalene*—according to Vasari, a replica of one promised to Philip in April but given instead to the nobleman Silvio Badoer.

1562. He finishes the *Christ in the Garden of Gethsemane* and *The Rape of Europa,* and sends them both to Spain. He sends Vecellio Vecelli di Pieve di Cadore a "picture of Adonis," by way of his son Orazio.

1563. On July 28, he assures Philip II that the *"Supper of Our Lord with the Twelve Apostles* seven cubits long and more than four high," started in 1558, is almost finished, and asks that he be given the pension in grain from Naples granted him some time previously by Charles V. However, the following year he has to give this pension up because, Garcia writes, "he could not remember, being old, where he had put the receipt."

1564. He sends Philip II the *Last Supper.* With his son Orazio, he goes into the timber trade, supplying the Duke of Urbino among others with wood. In October he goes to Brescia to see about the pending contract for three large vases to decorate the ceiling of the hall of the Palazzo Pubblico in that city, this ceiling having been decorated with perspectives by Cristoforo Rosa.

1565. With Cesare Vecellio, Emanuele da Augusta and Valerio Zuccato, he goes to Pieve di Cadore to give instructions about the execution, according to his drawings, of the frescoes in the apse of the archdiaconate in Pieve di Cadore.

1566. The Council of Ten grants Titian the monopoly of various prints which Cornelio Cort and Nicolò Baldrini were making from his paintings. On May 22, Giorgio Vasari arrives in Venice from Vicenza and Padua; he goes to pay homage to Titian in his Birri house and is able to make notes of the paintings in the artist's studio. Titian is elected a Member of the Academy of Tuscan Painters and, Sculptors together with other

Venetian artists, including Andrea Palladio and Tintoretto.

1567. He paints a *Mary Magdalene in the Desert,* a *St Peter the Martyr,* and a *St Catherine,* and sends them as gifts to Pius V, to Alessandro Farnese, and to Cardinal Alessandrino. In his letter of December 2 to Philip II, he assures the monarch that he has already finished *The Martyrdom of St Lawrence* which Vasari saw in 1566 when it was still in progress.

1568. The three ceiling canvases, finished in 1567, for the hall of the Palazzo Pubblico in Brescia are put in place. Titian assures Philip II that he has finished *The Tribute Money* now in the National Gallery, London. He offers to Maximilian II, by way of Strada and Veit von Dornberg (the Emperor's agent in Venice), versions—or models according to Tietze—of the following paintings already sent to Philip II: *Diana and Endymion, Diana and Callisto, Actaeon Torn to Pieces by the Dogs, Venus and Adonis, Perseus and Andromeda, The Rape of Europa.*

1569. At Titian's request, the Salt Brokerage Office is transferred to his son Orazio.

1570. Death of Sansovino on November 27. Alvise Mocenigo succeeds Pietro Loredan as Doge.

1571. Philip II approves the transferring of Titian's pension from the Milan Treasury to his son Orazio.

1573. Agatone notifies Duke Guidobaldo della Rocca on May 8 that Titian is finishing the painting of *Philip II Offering the Infante Don Fernando to Victory* which was commissioned by Philip II in 1571 in memory of the Battle of Lepanto on October 7, 1571.

1574. In a letter dated December 22, Titian lists for Antonio Perez, Philip II's secretary, the paintings sent to Spain—adding that he cannot remember them all—and asks for payment. Henry II visits Titian.

1575. He asks Philip II for payment of the works he has still not received money for, and in September sends to Spain the votive picture of the Battle of Lepanto, and *Spain Coming to the Aid of Religion* which had been seen by Vasari in 1566 while still in progress.

1576. FEBRUARY 26. This is the date of Titian's last letter asking the King of Spain for payment for his paintings. Titian dies on August 27, in his Birri house, while the plague is raging through Venice; he is buried on August 28 in the Church of the Frari. His favorite son Orazio dies a few days later, and the Birri house is abandoned and looted.

TITIAN'S PAINTINGS

Color Plate I

POPE PAUL III AND HIS GRAND-SONS ALESSANDRO AND OTTAVIO FARNESE. *Canvas, 210 × 174. Naples, Capodimonte.* Came from Palazzo del Giardino in Parma, where it is listed in the 1680 inventory (Campori, 1870). According to Vasari, it was painted in Rome in 1546 for the Farnese family.

Plate 1

POPE PAUL III AND HIS GRAND-SONS ALESSANDRO AND OTTAVIO FARNESE. Detail: the head of Ottavio Farnese.

Plate 2

PORTRAIT OF PAUL III WEARING THE PAPAL CAP. *Canvas (transferred in 1935 from the original canvas), 108 × 80. Naples, Capodimonte.* Came from Palazzo del Giardino in Parma, where it is listed in the 1680 inventory. Wickhoff makes a strange attribution to Paris Bordone, but the picture is generally considered to be a replica, painted by Titian's workshop, of the portrait of the Pope bareheaded (Part 2, plate 168). However, Berenson and Clausse (1905) do not agree. Even after the picture's 1935 restoration, Tietze-Conrat still believes it to be a replica —together with that in the Kunsthistorisches Museum in Vienna—of the painting formerly in the Barbarigo house and now in Leningrad (cf. plate 147a, Attributed Paintings). Ortolani (1948), on the other hand, holds that it was painted in Rome between 1545 and 1546, later than and based on the portrait of Julius II

copied from Raphael which is today in the Pitti Palace, and before the portrait of Paul III bareheaded which is also in Naples (cf. relevant note). Pallucchini, while he agrees that this canvas was painted in Rome, thinks a dating earlier than the other Naples portrait is very unlikely. (See also note to plate 168 in Part 2).

Plate 3

PORTRAIT OF CARDINAL ALESSANDRO FARNESE. *Canvas, 98 × 75. Naples, Capodimonte.* Formerly in the Farnese Palace in Rome, it was sent in 1662 to Parma where it is listed in the 1680 inventory of Palazzo del Giardino. Cavalcaselle, Ricketts, Fischel and Dussler (1935) doubt whether this portrait of Alessandro Farnese (1520–90), Cardinal of San Lorenzo and Damaso, is really an authentic Titian. It is accepted as such, however, by Berenson, Tietze (who believes it was painted either in Bologna in 1543 or in Rome in 1546) and Pallucchini (who tends to believe that it was painted during Titian's stay in Rome).

Plates 4–5

DANAË. *Canvas, 117 × 69. Naples, Capodimonte.* Came from Palazzo del Giardino in Parma, where it is listed in the 1680 inventory. According to Vasari, it was commissioned by Ottavio Farnese and painted in Rome in 1545–46. Tietze (1954), in publishing the *Danaë* in the Hickox Collection in New York (see plate 152, Attributed Paintings) as the first version of the canvas in Capodimonte in Naples, puts forward the theory that Titian began the Naples picture in Venice and finished it in Rome. There are many copies and replicas of the painting, some of them listed by Cavalcaselle.

Plate 6

PORTRAIT OF A GIRL. *Canvas, 84 × 75. Naples, Capodimonte*. Came from Palazzo del Giardino in Parma, where it is listed in the 1680 inventory. Because this painting belongs to the Farnese series, attempts have been made to identify the sitter as a member of the Farnese family, or as one of the young women frequenting their Court. It has also been suggested that the portrait is of Titia'ns daughter Lavinia. Dussler (1935) considers it to be a mediocre painting executed by Titian's workshop; Suida, Berenson and Pallucchini, among others, believe it to be an authentic Titian.

Plate 7

PORTRAIT OF PIER LUIGI FARNESE. *Canvas, 105 × 81. Naples, Capodimonte*. Formerly in the Farnese Palace in Rome, it was sent to Parma in September 1662 and is listed in the 1680 inventory of Palazzo del Giardino. Titian probably painted it in Venice in 1546, or possibly during his return journey to Venice from Rome (Cavalcaselle).

Plate 8

PORTRAIT OF A MAN WITH BOOK AND STAFF. *Canvas, 83 × 62. Vienna, Kunsthistorisches Museum*. Came from the Collection of the Archduke Leopold William. The book and the staff—which transform the portrait into a St James— are later additions, and, on the basis of a copy in the Berlin Museum, it can be seen that this painting and that of the

Boy (cf. plate 9), also in Vienna, together formed a single picture. This double portrait, now divided, is identified by Burckhard (1928 Catalog of the Museum) with that of Francesco Filetto and his son mentioned by Vasari. Bologna (1957) doubts this identification on the grounds that in Genoa there is a portrait attributed to Licinio and bearing the inscription "Franc. Philetus Doctor" in which the sitter's features differ notably from those of the adult portrayed in this Vienna canvas. The two portraits in the Kunsthistorisches Museum are generally dated 1545–48.

Color Plate II

PORTRAIT OF ISABELLA OF PORTUGAL (detail of plate 25).

Plate 9

PORTRAIT OF A BOY. *Canvas, 89 × 67. Vienna, Kunsthistorisches Museum*. Came from the Collection of the Archduke Leopold William. The arrows, attributes of St Sebastian, are a later addition (cf. note to plate 8).

Plate 10

PORTRAIT OF CARDINAL PIETRO BEMBO. *Canvas, 116 × 98. Naples, Capodimonte*. Cavalcaselle identifies this portrait with the one Titian painted before March 30, 1540 (cf. note to plate 159, Part 2); Pallucchini, however, attributes it to the artist's Roman period on stylistic grounds—but before 1547, the year of the Cardinal's death.

Plate 11

PORTRAIT OF PIETRO ARETINO. *Canvas, 99 × 82. New York, Frick Collection*. Formerly in the Chigi Palace in Rome. Suida dates it 1538; Tietze 1545; Mayer (1937), on the grounds that Aretino stopped dyeing his beard in 1548, believes the portrait was painted after this date. Most critics accept this canvas as an authentic Titian, but A. Venturi (among others) does not.

Plate 12
MADONNA AND CHILD IN GLORY, AND SS PETER AND PAUL. *Canvas, 456 × 270. Serravalle (Vittorio Veneto), Duomo.* Signed: TITIANVS. Originally commissioned from Francesco Vecellio, it was—on his advice—entrusted to Titian who painted it between 1542 and 1547. Although Ridolfi admired the picture greatly, extensive work by Titian's workshop is obvious.

Plate 13
ST JAMES OF COMPOSTELLA. *Canvas, 249 × 140. Venice, Church of San Lio.* Considerably enlarged on every side. It was believed to date from Titian's last period (Gronau), but since its restoration on the occasion of the Titian Exhibition in Venice (1935), it is now generally dated between 1540 and 1550—dates which Pallucchini narrows to 1547–48.

Plate 14
VOTIVE PORTRAIT OF THE VENDRAMIN FAMILY. *Canvas, 206 × 301. London, National Gallery.* Probably remained in Venice until 1636 (C. Gould, 1959), then passed to Van Dyck; from 1645 to 1646 it was the property of the Dukes of Northumberland from whom it was bought for the National Gallery in 1929. Once thought to be a portrait of the Cornaro family and dated 1560 (Cavalcaselle), it was identified by Gronau (1925) as Gabriele Vendramin surrounded by various members of his family, and dated by this critic about 1550—shortly before Gabriele's death in 1552. This 1550 date,

accepted by Tietze and Pallucchini, must be put back at least to 1547, because in that year Gabriele Vendramin drew up a will in favor of his brother Andrea and his sons, and Andrea and Leonardo Vendramin died—both of whom are portrayed in this picture (information volunteered by Admiral Aldo Bechis of Venice to Ferdinando Bologna, 1957; but cf. also C. Gould, 1959). See also plates 15–19.

Plate 15
VOTIVE PORTRAIT OF THE VENDRAMIN FAMILY. Detail: the crucifix and altar candles.

Plate 16
VOTIVE PORTRAIT OF THE VENDRAMIN FAMILY. Detail: the two men on the left with the children. From the left, kneeling: Bortolo (1530–84), Francesco (1529–70), Luca (1528–1601); and standing: Leonardo (1523–47), and Andrea (1481–1547) Vendramin.

Plate 17
VOTIVE PORTRAIT OF THE VENDRAMIN FAMILY. Detail: the children on the right with the little dog. From the left: Federico (1535–1611), Filippo (1534–1618), and Giovanni (1532–83) Vendramin.

Plate 18
VOTIVE PORTRAIT OF THE VENDRAMIN FAMILY. Detail: Gabriele Vendramin's right hand, with ring (1484–1552).

Plate 19
VOTIVE PORTRAIT OF THE VENDRAMIN FAMILY. Detail: Gabriele Vendramin's head.

Plate 20
ECCE HOMO. *Slate, 69 × 56. Madrid, Prado.* Signed: TITIANVS. Formerly

in the Escorial (1574) and the Alcazar (1600). Generally identified with the painting Titian took with him to Augsburg for Charles V in 1548, and of which he painted a replica for Pietro Aretino in 1547. Gronau does not believe that the entire painting is by Titian; Tietze lists the replicas in the Musée Condé in Chantilly and in the Ambrosiana in Milan.

Plate 21

PORTRAIT OF CHARLES V. *Canvas, 205 × 122. Munich, Bayerische Staatsgemäldesammlungen.* Signed and dated: TITIANVS F. MDXLVIII. Formerly in the Gallery of the Elector of Munich. Painted in Augsburg during Titian's first stay there, in 1548. Cavalcaselle sees in it the hand of Cesare Vecellio, while Ricketts, for some strange reason, believes it to have been painted by a Northern artist at the time of Rubens.

Plate 22

PORTRAIT OF CHARLES V AT THE BATTLE OF MÜHLBERG. *Canvas, 332 × 279. Madrid, Prado.* Came to Spain with Queen Marie of Hungary's inheritance. This is a commemorative portrait of the Battle of Mühlberg, fought on April 24, 1547, in which the Protestants were beaten on the banks of the Elbe. Painted in Augsburg between April and September 1548. Restored by C. Amberger shortly after it was finished (B. Beinert, 1946), it was badly damaged in the Alcazar fire of 1734. See also plates 23 and 24.

Plate 23

PORTRAIT OF CHARLES V AT THE BATTLE OF MÜHLBERG. Detail: the Emperor's head.

Plate 24

PORTRAIT OF CHARLES V AT THE BATTLE OF MÜHLBERG. Detail: the horse's head.

Plate 25

PORTRAIT OF ISABELLA OF PORTUGAL. *Canvas, 117 × 93. Madrid, Prado.* Listed in the 1686 inventory of the Alcazar, this is in all probability the portrait of Charles V's wife Isabella, who died in 1539 in Toledo, which Titian painted during his first stay in Augsburg (G. Glück, 1933; Beroqui, 1946), rather than that sent by Don Diego Hurtado de Mendoza on October 5, 1545 (see Lost Paintings, Part 2, p. 112).

Plate 26

PORTRAIT OF NICOLAS PERRENOT GRANVELLA. *Canvas, 122 × 93. Besançon, Musée des Beaux-Arts.* Formerly the property of the Granvella family. Although Cavalcaselle and other critics may think in terms of an unknown painter influenced by Titian, and A. Venturi (*Storia dell'Arte*, 1929, VII) in terms of Scipione Pulzone, this portrait is identifiable as the one Titian painted in Augsburg in 1548 of this great statesman who was Secretary to Charles V and President of the Diet.

Plate 27

PORTRAIT OF ANTONIO PERRENOT GRANVELLA. *Canvas, 112 × 86.5. Kansas City (Missouri), Gallery of Art, W. Rockill Nelson Collection.* Signed: TITIANVS DE CADORE. Formerly in the B. A. Tattorn Collection. Partly on the evidence of an external detail—the pendulum clock of the type made in Augsburg (Gronau, 1922)—it is possible to date this portrait of Nicola de Granvella's son in all probability to Titian's first stay in Augsburg (1548).

Plate 28

PORTRAIT OF GIOVANNI DA CAS-
TALDO. *Canvas,* 113.2 × 94.
Geneva, private collection. According to
Vasari, this portrait was painted in
Augsburg in 1548 (Tietze).

Plate 29

PORTRAIT OF JOHN FREDERICK
OF SAXONY. *Canvas,* 103.5 × 83.
Vienna, Kunsthistorisches Museum. The
identification of this picture with the
portrait which belonged to Queen
Marie of Hungary and which then
passed to Vienna in 1556 is uncertain
(see p. 70, Lost Paintings). The
canvas was already in the Imperial
Gallery in Vienna in 1720, and is
considered to be a painting Titian
executed in Augsburg either in 1548
or in 1550–51, when the Great
Elector John Frederick of Saxony,
leader of the Protestant forces
beaten at Mühlberg in 1547, was in
the city as Charles V's prisoner.
Wickhoff (1904) believes it to be a
copy by Rubens of a Titian painting;
Ricketts thinks that the artist must
have had in mind a portrait by a
Northern painter when he executed
this picture.

Plate 30

PROMETHEUS. *Canvas,* 253 × 217.
Madrid, Prado. Mentioned by Dolce
and by Vasari, this and two other
paintings representing Tantalus and
Sisyphus were seen by Calvette de
Estrella in August 1549 in Binche
(Flanders), the summer residence of
Queen Marie of Hungary, who had
commissioned the pictures from
Titian in Augsburg in 1548. A
fourth painting in the series called
"of the Damned" or "of the Furies,"
representing Ixion, was sent to
Flanders in 1553 (Tietze). Of these
four paintings, which were taken to
Spain in 1556 after the sacking of the
Binche Palace, only the two repre-
senting Tityus (Prometheus) and
Sisyphus are today preserved in the
Prado—and, what is more, even
these were considered by older
Spanish writers to be copies (Beroqui, 1946). See plate 31 and p. 72,
Lost Paintings.

Plate 31

SISYPHUS. *Canvas,* 237 × 216.
Madrid, Prado. See note to plate 30.

Plate 32

VENUS, CUPID AND AN ORGANIST.
Canvas, 148 × 217. *Madrid, Prado.*
Signed: TITIANVS F. Listed in the
Alcazar in 1636. Usually identified
with the "Venus on a bed with an
organ player" painted in August
1548 for Granvella. Sold to Rudolf
II, then sent by him to Philip III of
Spain (Beroqui, 1946). Suida considers this to be a genuine Titian in
its entirety; other critics such as
Gronau and Tietze hold it was
mostly painted by Titian's workshop.
Berenson and Pallucchini think the
workshop's part is of minor importance.

Plate 33

VENUS AND AN ORGANIST. *Canvas,*
136 × 220. *Madrid, Prado.* Noted
for the first time in the 1686 inventory of the Alcazar. Hadeln (1931)
puts forward the hypothesis that this
is the painting executed for Francesco Assonica which came into
Philip IV's possession when it was
purchased from Charles I of England.
This *Venus,* which is later than the
preceding one (plate 32), is also
believed by Suida to be a genuine
Titian, whereas Tietze thinks that
Titian's workshop predominates.

Plate 34

VENUS, CUPID, AN ORGANIST
AND A LITTLE DOG. *Canvas,* 115 ×
280. *Berlin, Staatliche Museen.* Signed:

TITIANVS F. Possibly still in Italy in the eighteenth century, in the Collection of Prince Pio of Savoia (Suida, 1957). Came to the Berlin Museum by purchase in 1915 (W. Bode, 1917–18). According to Strong (*Journal of Roman Studies*, 27, p. 118), the Cupid caressing Venus is based on a classic model. Datable about 1550, it is one of the versions of this subject in which the intervention of Titian's workshop is less noticeable.

Plate 35
VENUS, CUPID AND A LITTLE DOG. *Canvas, 119 × 195. Florence, Uffizi.* Offered by Paolo Giordano Orsini to Cosimo II in 1618; then in the Collection of Antonio de' Medici and from there to the Uffizi by bequest in 1632. Generally dated to about 1545 (Gronau, Suida), it is thought to have been painted after 1550 according to Berenson. Pallucchini prefers this later date, and quite rightly considers the picture to have been partly painted by Titian's workshop.

Plate 36
ST TITIAN. *Canvas, 180 × 59. Lentiai (Belluno), Parish Church.* This is the only compartment of the big Lentiai polyptych which Titian painted entirely on his own. The remainder of the polyptych comprises: *The Assumption* in the center, with full-length figures of saints at the sides—*St Titian and St Peter* on the left and *St John the Evangelist and St Paul* on the right; above is the *Pietà*, and half-figures of saints— *Victor and Corona and Mary Magdalene and Anthony Abbot.* The polyptych was painted by Titian's workshop, with the participation of Francesco Vecellio (F. Valcanover, 1951). Ticozzi (1817) attributes it to Marco Vecellio, Vergerio (1931) to Cesare Vecellio; Cavalcaselle feels he can see the intervention of Francesco,

Marco and Cesare Vecellio. Pallucchini, who holds that the figure of *St Titian* is by Titian himself, attributed the rest of the polyptych to Orazio Vecellio by comparing it with the small doors of the parish church in Calalzo—which are, however, much inferior in quality. The polyptych may be dated slightly later than that at Castello Roganzuolo, at the end of the fifth decade of the sixteenth century (cf. note to plate 159, Attributed Paintings).

Plate 37
MATER DOLOROSA. *Panel, 68 × 61. Madrid, Prado.* Charles V took this picture with him when he went into voluntary exile in Juste, and it was transferred to the Escorial after his death. It is probably the painting Titian handed over, with others, to the Emperor in Augsburg in 1550. Mayer (1935), in dating the panel to 1548, makes known a second version of it, in the Museo Cerralbo in Madrid, which he believes to have been executed before 1560.

Plate 38
SUPPOSED PORTRAIT OF BENEDETTO VARCHI. *Canvas, 117 × 91. Vienna, Kunsthistorisches Museum.* Signed: TITIANVS F. Formerly in the Collection of the Archduke Leopold William, 1659. The traditional identification of the sitter as Benedetto Varchi, based on a medallion by Domenico Paggini, is doubted by Cavalcaselle, Gronau, Suida and Pallucchini—this last critic dating the portrait to about 1550 or later. Those critics who do accept the Benedetto Varchi identification put back the date of the painting to 1536–43, the years in which Varchi, the teacher of the Strozzi family, took refuge in Venice. Tietze, while uncertain about the traditional identification of the

portrait, proposes a date of about 1543 for its execution.

Plate 39

PORTRAIT OF ANTONIO ANSELMI. *Canvas, 70 × 63.5. Lugano, Thyssen Collection.* On the reverse, a later inscription which reads: (ANT)ONIUS ANSELMUS ANN. XXXVIII. MDL (T)ITI-ANUS F. Formerly in Berlin in the Diercksen Collection. Rintelen (1905), Suida, Tietze and Pallucchini, among others, accept this as an authentic Titian with a date of 1550.

Plate 40

PORTRAIT OF A GENTLEMAN. *Canvas, 223 × 151. Kassel, Gemälde-galerie.* Once thought to be the portrait of Alfonso d'Avalos. Justi thought he could identify it as that of Giovanni Francesco Acquaviva, Duke of Atri; however, this identification is not borne out by a comparison with the portrait which is definitely of the Duke of Atri and which was found by Hadeln (1934). Cavalcaselle dates it about 1550 and this date is generally accepted by critics today. See also plate 41.

Color Plate III

PORTRAIT OF PHILIP II (detail of plate 43).

Plate 41

PORTRAIT OF A GENTLEMAN. Detail: the dog.

Plate 42

PORTRAIT OF PHILIP II. *Canvas, 131.3 × 93.7. Cincinnati, Museum of Art.* Came from the Barbarigo-Giustiniani Collection in Padua. Formerly in the Lenbach Collection in Munich and the Thomas J. Emery Collection in Cincinnati. According to Mayer (1925), it may be dated to 1556, later than the picture in the Rasch Collection in Stockholm (cf. note to plate 49) which Beroqui

(1946) and Berenson identify as the "very rapid sketch" executed by Titian in Milan between December 20 and January 7, 1549, while the Cincinnati painting would be the copy which Granvella, Bishop of Arras, requested from Titian on April 23, 1549. Tietze-Conrat (1946) and Pallucchini, on the other hand, believe that the Stockholm portrait is derived from this Cincinnati one. Tietze tends to consider it the "model," dating about 1554, which remained in Titian's workshop and which served for many replicas, that of the Rasch Collection among them.

Plate 43

PORTRAIT OF PHILIP II. *Canvas, 193 × 111. Madrid, Prado.* Painted during the second visit to Augsburg, in February 1551, and sent the same year to Queen Marie of Hungary who was in the Low Countries. Transferred to London after Philip's marriage in 1554 to Mary Tudor, it came back into the possession of Marie of Hungary, and she took it with her two years later when she went to Spain (Beroqui, 1946). See also plate 44.

Plate 44

PORTRAIT OF PHILIP II. Detail: the head.

Plate 45

SUPPOSED PORTRAIT OF A KNIGHT OF MALTA. *Canvas, 122 × 101. Madrid, Prado.* At one time believed to be by Tintoretto (1666 inventory of the Alcazar), but already attributed to Titian in the 1747 inventories. Babelon (in *Revue de l'Art ancien et moderne*, 1913) thinks it portrays Giannello della Torre, clock-maker to Charles V and Philip II; Salazar and Sanchez Canton (1919)—who remark that the white cross is not that of the Order of Malta—believe it to be the portrait of a gentleman of the Cuccina family. Beroqui (1946) does not find either of these identifications probable. Most critics accept 1550 as the date of execution.

Plate 46a

PORTRAIT OF MARTINO PASQUA-LIGO. *Canvas, 78.4 × 63.2. Washington, D.C. Corcoran Gallery of Art.* Signed: TICIANUS, it bears the following inscription: MARTINUS PAS-QUALIGUS STATUARIUS VENETUS. Suida and Tietze date it 1554–55 and identify it with the portrait of Pasqualigo the sculptor which Ridolfi mentions as being in the house of Bortolo Dofino. Pallucchini sees in it the intervention of Titian's workshop.

Plate 46b

PORTRAIT OF A FRIEND OF TITIAN. *Canvas, 87.5 × 70. San Francisco, De Young Memorial Museum.* On the paper in the sitter's left hand is written: "*Di Titiano Vecellio Singolare Amico*" ("Titian Vecellio's personal friend"). Formerly in the Lansdowne and Frank Sabin Collections in London. Suida (1933) dated it 1530; then 1540 (in 1955); Wilde (1934) about 1540; Tietze and Pallucchini about 1550. In a painting which was executed by Titian's workshop and which is now in the Royal Collection in Hampton Court (S. J. Gore, 1958), the same man is portrayed together with Titian and Andrea de' Franceschi. None of the various identifications suggested, fascinating though they may be, have any real historical foundation (Borenius, 1937; Suida, 1955).

Plate 47a

PORTRAIT OF LUDOVICO BECCA-DELLI. *Canvas, 111 × 98.5. Florence, Uffizi.* The paper the sitter holds bears the inscription: "*Julius P.P. III Venerabili frati Ludovico Episcopo Ravellen, apud Dominum Venetorum nostro et Apostolicae sedis Nuntio, cum annum ageret LII, Titianus Vecellius faciebat Venetiis MDLII mense Julii.*" In the Collection of Cardinal Leopoldo de' Medici, purchased in 1675. Mentioned in a letter and a sonnet of Pietro Aretino's in October 1552, the year in which Beccadelli was Papal Legate to Venice.

Plate 47b

PORTRAIT OF A FRANCISCAN MONK. *Canvas, 82.5 × 2.5. Melbourne, National Gallery of Victoria.* Hadeln (1924), and Pallucchini, date it about 1550, as does Tietze, who feels that this date is more plausible than 1560–70, suggested by Fischel.

Plate 48

PORTRAIT OF PHILIP II. *Canvas, 187 × 100. Naples, Capodimonte.* Signed: TITIANUS EQUES CAES F. Listed in the 1626 inventory of the inheritance of Odoardo Farnese in Caprarola; then in 1652 it passed from the Farnese Palace in Rome to Palazzo del Giardino in Parma, where it may be identified with a portrait of Philip described in the works transferred by Carlo III from Parma to Naples in 1698 (F. Bologna, 1954). Mayer (1925) and Tietze consider it the best replica painted by Titian's workshop of the portrait Titian sent in March 1553 to Prince Philip (which Beroqui—1946—doubts was a full-length portrait) and which is generally thought to be lost; Cavalcaselle, Gronau, Berenson and Pallucchini believe this Naples portrait is the original one. The painting in the Pitti Palace, which Vasari mentions as hanging in the "dressing-room" of Grand Duke Cosimo I, is quite rightly thought to be a derivation painted by Titian's workshop of this Naples portrait. (See also Lost Paintings, p. 73, and Attributed Paintings, p. 86.)

Color Plate IV
DANAË (detail of plate 58).

Plate 49
PORTRAIT OF PHILIP II. *Canvas, 96 × 75. Stockholm, Rasch Collection.* Formerly in the Habich Collection in Kassel and the Lenbach Collection in Munich. Zarnowski (1938) attributes it to Girolamo di Tiziano. According to Mayer (1925), it may be dated three years earlier than the Cincinnati version—which he dates 1556 (cf. note to plate 42). Tietze-Conrat (1946), on the other hand, considers it one of the versions which Titian himself painted of the picture in Cincinnati. Pallucchini favors Tietze-Conrat's hypothesis, and, since Philip is portrayed with a scepter in his hand, thinks 1554 is a probable date for the picture's execution—this being the year in which Charles V's son was elected King of Naples and the Two Sicilies on the occasion of his marriage to Mary Tudor, Queen of England—or otherwise 1555, at the time of Charles V's retirement to Juste.

Plate 50
PORTRAIT OF THE DOGE FRAN-CESCO VENIER. *Canvas, 113 × 99. Lugano, Thyssen Collection.* Formerly in Prince Trivulzio's Collection. Tietze does not mention it, but Hadeln (1930), Suida and Pallucchini all quite rightly consider it a genuine Titian, and identify the sitter as the Doge Francesco Venier (1554–56), whose official portrait Titian had painted in 1555.

Plate 51
PORTRAIT OF THE DOGE FRAN-CESCO VENIER. Detail: the landscape.

Plate 52
ST MARGARET AND THE DRAGON. *Canvas, 210 × 170. Escorial, Monastery of St Lawrence.* Identified by Beroqui (1946) and M. Lorente Junquera (1951) with the painting Titian mentions in one of his letters dated October 11, 1552, as having been sent shortly before to Philip II. Cavalcaselle, on the other hand, thinks this latter picture is the one on the same subject now in the Prado. Cf. plate 113.

Plate 53
THE ADORATION OF THE HOLY TRINITY. *Canvas, 346 × 240. Madrid, Prado.* Signed: TITIANUS P. On the right-hand side, towards the top, Charles V, the Empress Isabella, Philip II and Queen Marie of Hungary are portrayed praying. Begun in 1551 and sent to Charles V in Flanders before October 1554. Charles took it with him to Juste in 1555, and on his death it was transferred to the Escorial. The painting in the National Gallery in London, generally considered to be a preparatory study for this large picture (Holmes, 1927), is quite rightly believed by Mayer to be a copy. Cort's engraving in 1566 based on a drawing by Titian differs in many respects from the Prado painting (on this question, cf. C. Gould, 1959).

Plate 54
BUST OF CHRIST. *Canvas, 68 × 62. Madrid, Prado.* Listed in the Escorial from 1574 on. This is all that is left of the "Christ appearing to Mary Magdalene" which Titian painted in 1553 on a commission from Queen

Marie of Hungary and sent to Flanders in the autumn of 1554 (cf. Lost Paintings, 1553–54, *Noli me tangere*). A second version—possibly the model for this Prado one (Tietze) —was seen in Titian's studio by Vasari in 1566.

Plate 55

MATER DOLOROSA. *Marble, 63 × 53. Madrid, Prado*. Bears the partial signature: TITIAN . . . S. Sent to Charles V with *The Adoration of the Holy Trinity* (plate 53) in October 1554. Tietze notes another version with variations in the Carvalho Collection in Paris.

Plate 56

VENUS AND ADONIS. *Canvas, 175 × 188. London, National Gallery*. Formerly in the Colonna Palace in Rome, then in London in the Angerstein Collection. Purchased for the National Gallery in 1824. Datable about 1554. Holmes's (1924) and Mayer's hypothesis—that this is the model which remained for a long time in Titian's workshop, and which was acquired by Tintoretto on Titian's death—is accepted by Tietze-Conrat (1946) and by Pallucchini (C. Gould, 1959).

Plate 57

VENUS AND ADONIS. *Canvas, 185 × 207. Madrid, Prado*. Painted in 1553 for Prince Philip and described by Dolce, it arrived on September 10 of the following year in London— where the Prince married Mary Tudor, Queen of England (Mayer, 1925).

Plate 58

DANAË. *Canvas, 128 × 178. Madrid, Prado*. It is one of the "poesies" which Titian assured Philip II he was working on in 1553, and then sent him the next year (Cavalcaselle).

Plate 59

DANAË. *Canvas, 119.5 × 187. Leningrad, Hermitage*. In France in the Collection of the Marquis De Vrillière, Secretary of State, in 1633; then in the Thevenin Collection. Purchased from the Crozat Collection. L. Venturi (1912) and the Tietzes (1954 and 1956) consider it a replica, painted by Titian's workshop, of the Madrid painting; Gronau, Berenson and Pallucchini, among others, rightly attribute it to Titian himself about 1554—even though his workshop probably collaborated.

Plate 60

DANAË. *Canvas, 138 × 152. Vienna, Kunsthistorisches Museum*. Signed: TITIANVS AEQUES CAES. Acquired in Rome by Cardinal Montalto for the Emperor Rudolf II's Collection, it is another version, with variations, of the Prado *Danaë* (plate 58). It is generally considered to have been painted mostly by Titian's workshop (Berenson), and is not included in Tietze's lists. However, Pallucchini quite rightly feels that much of it was painted by Titian himself.

Plate 61

PORTRAIT OF A GIRL. *Canvas, 102 × 86. Dresden, Gemäldegalerie*. From the Ducal Collection in Modena, where it is listed by Scannelli (1657) as "Titian's mistress." Hadeln (1931) refutes both this identification and that with Lavinia, Titian's daughter, which Cavalcaselle puts forward and which is accepted by Gronau and Berenson. Some critics wrongly consider this to be a copy of a lost original; Tietze and Pallucchini, among others, believe it to be a genuine Titian, and this latter critic thinks that it probably dates from about 1555.

Plate 62

VENUS WITH A MIRROR. *Canvas, 124.5 × 105.5. Washington, D.C., National Gallery of Art, Mellon Collection.* Came from Titian's bequest to the Barbarigo family in 1581, was ceded by them to the Hermitage in St Petersburg, and was later bought by Mellon. It may be dated 1555, and is the only version among the many pictures on the basic theme (with variations from picture to picture) of Venus looking in the mirror which is undoubtedly an authentic Titian. Poglayen Neuwall, who has written on the subject several times (1929, 1934, 1947), distinguishes three different types of composition. 1: "*Venus pudica,*" nude, "at the mirror with two Cupids," of which the prototype, he says, is the lost painting mentioned by Ridolfi in Venice in the house of Nicolò Crasso, the jurist. From this painting he claims both the Washington version and the replica in the Buchenau (formerly Nemes) Collection (which is not, however, by Titian) derive—and on them, in turn, are based the old copies in the Hermitage (attributed to Orazio Vecellio), in the Moscow Fine Arts Museum, in Lord Ashburton's Collection (now lost—Cavalcaselle feels this one is in the style of Padovanino), and in the possession of Mrs Wakefield. 1b: "*Venus pudica* at the mirror with one Cupid only." Variants of this type of the "*Crasso Venus*" would be the old copies in the Kassel Gemäldegalerie (signed Gillis Congnet), in Hampton Court (formerly in Charles I's Collection), in the Sansouci Gallery in Potsdam, and in the Italian Embassy in London (formerly in the Gualino Collection—in this one, however, the Venus is transformed into a Leda). From the Washington *Venus*, Neuwall claims would be derived the copies in the Dresden Art Gallery (two versions),

in the Czartoryscky Collection in Cracow (lost), in the Bergsten Collection formerly in Stockholm, and in the Berlin Museum. From the *Venus*, formerly in the Nemes Collection, Munich, would be derived the other copies in the Art Gallery of the Academy in Vienna, in the Magdeburg Museum (by David Teniers the Younger), in the H. Schwaneck Collection in Munich. 2a: "*Venus genetrix*, at the mirror with a Cupid." From the lost prototype, which Poglayen Neuwall identifies in the "Venus with Cupid holding her mirror" mentioned by Titian in his famous letter of 1574 to Philip II (see Lost Paintings, 1574), would be derived the paintings in Viscount Lee of Fareham's Collection in Richmond, in a private collection in Partenkirchen, and in the San Luca Gallery in Rome. 2b: "*Venus pudica*" but with characteristics of the "*Venus genetrix.*" Late copies in the Cordon Collection in Brussels, in the Art Gallery in Augsburg, and in the Corsini Gallery in Rome. 3: "*Venus pudica*" alone. To this group, which takes up the motif of the "*Crasso Venus,*" belong (according to Poglayen Neuwall) the late versions in the Castle of Charlottenburg, in the Residenz Museum in Munich, in Berlin, and also the "Venus of the Ca' d'Oro" in Venice, which, after its recent restoration, appears to be of such high quality as to make one think Titian himself executed much of it. (See note on p. 92, Attributed Paintings: *Venus.*)

Plate 63

GIRL WITH DISH OF FRUIT. *Canvas, 102 × 82. Berlin, Staatliche Museen.* Acquired by Abbot Celotti in Florence in 1832. The painting, in which Cavalcaselle believes he can detect the collaboration of Orazio

Vecellio, was for a long time thought to be the portrait of Titian's daughter Lavinia. Hadeln (1931), in refuting this identification, quite rightly considers the picture a late version of the series of half-length feminine figures. It is generally dated about 1555 (Tietze).

Plate 64

THE RISEN CHRIST APPEARING TO HIS MOTHER. *Canvas, 276 × 198. Medole (Mantua), Church of Santa Maria.* Badly damaged during the disorders which followed the French Revolution. Probably painted in 1554, the year in which Titian asked the Duke of Mantua to transfer the Canonry of Medole from his son Pomponio, who as time went on was less and less inclined to an ecclesiastical career, to one of his nephews (Cavalcaselle). The collaboration of his workshop in this picture is obvious (Pallucchini).

Plate 65

ST JEROME IN THE WILDERNESS. *Canvas, 255 × 125. Milan, Brera.* Signed: TICIANUS F. The curved upper part is a later addition. Came at the beginning of the nineteenth century from the Church of Santa Maria Nuova in Venice, where it is mentioned by Ridolfi. Cavalcaselle dates it after 1560. Gronau, 1550, Tietze, 1552; the majority of art critics agree with Tietze.

Plate 66

THE MARTYRDOM OF ST LAW-RENCE. *Canvas (transferred from the original canvas in 1873), 500 × 280. Venice, Church of the Jesuits.* During its recent restoration (1959), the signature: TITIANUS VECELLIUS AEQUES F. has been found to be in a later and different hand. Titian was working

on it by November 18, 1548, as a commission from Lorenzo Massolo to decorate his tomb in the Church of the Crociferi (now of the Jesuits), but had still not handed it over by March 15, 1557, when Massolo was already dead. It was in place in 1559 (R. Gallo, 1935). It is probable, therefore, that Titian had worked on it immediately after his return from Rome and before leaving for Augsburg in 1548. A study of the executioner in the right foreground is to be found in the Uffizi (charcoal pencil, heightened in white, 40.3 × 25.3) and is reproduced here. See also plates 67, 68, 69 and 121.

Plate 67

THE MARTYRDOM OF ST LAW-RENCE. Detail: the group of executioners to the left, and of the Saint.

Plate 68

THE MARTYRDOM OF ST LAW-
RENCE. Detail: the statue and of the
torch on the left, above.

Plate 69

THE MARTYRDOM OF ST LAW-
RENCE. Detail: the head of the
soldier carrying the flag.

Plate 70

PENTECOST. *Canvas, 570 × 260.
Venice, Church of Santa Maria della
Salute.* Painted for the Church of
Santo Spirito in Isola to take the
place of an earlier picture which was
already in place in 1541 but which
was ruined very soon afterwards,
according to Vasari (cf. Lost Paintings, 1541, *Pentecost*). Usually dated
about 1555 (Fogolari, 1935; Pallucchini). Tietze, however, dates it
about 1560.

Plate 71

THE ANNUNCIATION. *Canvas, 232
× 190. Naples, Church of San
Domenico Maggiore.* Signed: TITIANVS
FECIT. Mentioned in 1623 (*Napoli
sacra*) by D'Eugenio, according to
whom the chapel where the altarpiece is placed was consecrated in
1557. According to De Dominici
(*Vite...*, 1742), it was removed and
a copy by Luca Giordano put in its
place. After this presumed substitu-
tion, the painting was ignored by art
critics, but in 1925, R. Longhi
proved that it was certainly an
authentic Titian. Datable 1557
(Tietze) or soon after (Pallucchini).

Plate 72

VENUS WITH THE LUTE PLAYER.
*Canvas, 157 × 205. New York, Metro-
politan Museum.* Probably remained
in Italy up to the early eighteenth
century. According to the inventories of Holkham House, it was
bought in Rome from the Collection

of Prince Pio of Savoy. Purchased
from the Holkham House Collection
in 1936. It is considered to be an
authentic Titian by Gronau, Berenson, Richter (1931), L. Venturi
(1933), Brendel (1946), Pallucchini,
and, more recently, by Suida (1957).
According to Hadeln (1932), it
was completed in 1560, but begun
many years earlier. Suida (1957) dates
it about 1560 and after, and thinks
that there is no historical connection
which would uphold the identification which Tietze-Conrat suggests
(1944) between this picture and the
painting on a similar subject mentioned by Sandrart as a work by
Domenico Tintoretto.

Plate 73

VENUS AND A LUTE PLAYER.
*Canvas, 151.7 × 186.8. Cambridge,
Fitzwilliam Museum.* Formerly in the
Collection of the Emperor Rudolf II
(1566–1612) as a work by Titian, it
was then carried off by the Swedish
troops in 1648 and transferred to the
Collection of Queen Christina. It
then passed into the Gallery of the
Duke of Orléans, and was bought
from the gallery in 1798 by Lord
Fitzwilliam. It is another version of
the New York Metropolitan Museum
painting (plate 72)—inferior in
quality according to Pallucchini.
Suida (1957), on the other hand,
followed by Studdert-Kennedy
(1958), believes it to be a replica
painted by Titian himself.

Plate 74

THE CRUCIFIXION, WITH THE
VIRGIN, SS DOMINIC AND JOHN.
*Canvas, 330 × 190. Ancona, Church of
San Domenico.* Signed: TICIANVS
FECIT. Mentioned by Vasari, it was
placed above the altar on July 22,
1558 (R. Elia, "La Parrocchia di S.
Domenico," in *Numero unico in
omaggio al nuovo Parroco...*, Ancona,

1939). Before this information was made known, the picture was dated between 1560 (Gronau) and 1563 (Cavalcaselle).

Plate 75

ST JEROME. *Canvas, 184 × 170. Escorial, Monastery of St Lawrence.* Signed: TITIANVS F. Correctly dated by Longhi (1946) about 1560, this is probably the painting which Titian sent to Philip II on September 24, 1575. Tietze doubts this is a genuine Titian. Pallucchini accepts the Titian attribution and puts forward the hypothesis that the landscape was painted at the time the picture was sent to Philip II. (See Lost Paintings, 1575.)

Plate 76

THE ADORATION OF THE MAGI. *Canvas, 138 × 222. Escorial, Monastery of St Lawrence.* Listed in the Escorial in 1574. Cavalcaselle thinks it was painted by a Spanish artist. It is, however, to be identified with the painting probably executed in 1559, and sent to Philip II in the following year (A. L. Mayer, 1937; Beroqui, 1946). Pallucchini does not exclude the possibility of collaboration by Titian's workshop—which painted almost all of the version in the Prado in Madrid which was once thought to be the painting sent to Spain in 1560 (cf. plate 172, Attributed Paintings).

Plate 77

THE ADORATION OF THE MAGI. *Canvas, 118 × 222. Milan, Ambrosiana.* Formerly the property of Cardinal Federigo Borromeo who bought it from the Ospedale Maggiore in Milan. Described in the donation document (1618), when Cardinal Federigo Borromeo's Collection was given to the Ambrosiana, as commissioned from Titian by Cardinal Ippolito d'Este of Ferrara so that he might give it as a present to Henry II, King of France, then as coming into the possession of St Charles Borromeo who bequeathed it to the Ospedale Maggiore in Milan. According to Mayer (1937), it is a second version of the subject, with variations in the background more than elsewhere, of the Escorial painting (plate 76). Cavalcaselle is reminded of the styles of Schiavone and Jacopo Bassano; Tietze considers the work a characteristic one painted by Titian's workshop; Berenson and Suida quite rightly believe it to be largely by Titian himself. The version mentioned by Mayer (1937) in the Atri Collection in Paris (cf. p. 92, Attributed Paintings) is certainly a replica painted by Titian's workshop. Tietze-Conrat (1954) believes she can identify the picture painted for Ippolito d'Este with that in the Walter Luthy Collection in Aarburg, Switzerland (cf. plate 170, Attributed Paintings). See also plate 78.

Plate 78

THE ADORATION OF THE MAGI. Detail: the figures on the left.

Plate 79

THE ENTOMBMENT. *Canvas, 137 × 185. Madrid, Prado.* Signed: TITIANVS VECELLVS AEQUES CAES. Commissioned in January 1559, it was sent to Philip II in the autumn of the same year, in place of another version of half-figure size which had disappeared in transit. Wickhoff (1909) doubts—without reason—the Titian attribution, and ascribes the picture to Palma Giovane. According to Foscari (1935), Titian has made the figure of St Joseph of Arimathea into a self-portrait.

44

Plate 80

WISDOM. *Canvas, 169 × 169.
Venice, Sansoviniana Library.* Mentioned by Ridolfi and Boschini, it was probably painted shortly after 1559, the year in which Titian (on September 9), was asked to evaluate the decorations in perspective painted by Rosa (Crowe-Cavalcaselle), who had been delegated to paint the central compartment as well in 1560 (Fogolari, 1935). Pallucchini quite rightly reaffirms that this is an authentic Titian, over Tietze's doubts on the subject. This critic believes the hexagon was painted by Titian's workshop. See also plate 81.

Plate 81

WISDOM. Detail: the bust.

Plate 82

SALOME. *Canvas, 87 × 80. Madrid, Prado.* Purchased in 1665 from the estate of the Marquis de' Laganes. It is a replica (with the head of John the Baptist on the platter instead of fruit) of the Berlin half-figure (plate 63). Tietze believes it was painted by Titian's workshop; Suida, Berenson and Pallucchini (among others) consider it to be an authentic Titian.

Plate 83

THE STONING OF ST STEPHEN. *Canvas, 194 × 121. Lille, Musée des Beaux-Arts.* In spite of the fact that this canvas has been correctly reappraised as a Titian by R. Longhi (1946), it is still attributed to Tintoretto in the catalog of the "Exhibition of Masterpieces from the Lille Museum" held in Ghent in 1950—although this catalog does note that Demmler had attributed the painting to Titian, while Hadeln had thought in terms of an artist in the old Titian's circle—possibly Damiano Mazza (Pallucchini).

Plate 84

DIANA AND ACTAEON. *Canvas, 190.5 × 207. Edinburgh, National Gallery of Scotland, on loan from the Earl of Ellesmere, 1955.* Signed: TITIANVS F. This picture, together with the following one depicting *Diana and Callisto* (plate 85) was begun in 1556 and sent to Philip II at the end of the summer in 1559. These two "compositions" were offered by Philip IV at the beginning of the eighteenth century to the Duke of Grammont who transferred them to France, where they entered the Gallery of the Duke of Orléans. They were then taken to England.

Plate 85

DIANA AND CALLISTO. *Canvas, 187 × 205. Edinburgh, National Gallery of Scotland, on loan from the Earl of Ellesmere, 1955.* Signed: TITIANVS F. Cf. note to plate 84. Restored in 1933, as was the preceding picture (R. Fry and K. North, 1933). In the Prado, two smaller copies (96 × 107) are to be found which were at one time attributed to Titian; Madrazo (various editions of the Prado Catalog) and

Cavalcaselle, however, attribute them to Mazo. A drawing in charcoal pencil (22.5 × 26.5) by Titian, possibly depicting *Jove and Io*, to be found in the Fitzwilliam Museum in Cambridge and datable from this same period, is here reproduced.

Plate 86

DIANA AND CALLISTO. *Canvas, 182 × 201. Vienna, Kunsthistorisches Museum.* Formerly in the Collection of the Archduke Leopold William. Cavalcaselle believes it to have been painted by Titian's workshop, and assumes Orazio and Girolamo or Andrea Schiavone helped; Fischer, Stix (1913), Suida and Tietze all consider it a replica by Titian himself of the Ellesmere painting which is now in Edinburgh (plate 85). During the picture's restoration, a preparatory drawing came to light which is similar in every respect with the Ellesmere canvas, but which was probably drawn by one of Titian's helpers: Girolamo di Tiziano, according to Zarnowski (1938). From this, Pallucchini deduces Titian contributed when the painting was nearing completion not only in the landscape and fountain, but also in the final layers of painting.

Plate 87

DIANA AND ACTAEON. *Canvas, 179 × 189. London, Earl of Harewood's Collection on loan to the National Gallery.* This is most probably the painting described as still unfinished in one of Titian's letters to Philip II in 1559. Formerly in the Collections of Queen Christina of Sweden (1689), of the Azzolini and Odescalchi families, and then of the Dukes of Orléans (1721), it became the property of Sir A. Hume and Lord Alford, and was then bought by Colnaghi from the Earl of Brownlow. Most critics believe this is an authentic Titian, but Hetzer (1940) doubts the attribution and feels the picture was painted by an unknown artist who also should be credited with *The Annunciation* in San Domenico Maggiore in Naples (plate 71).

Plate 88

THE RAPE OF EUROPA. *Canvas, 185 × 205. Boston, Isabella Stewart Gardner Museum.* Signed: TITIANVS F. At the beginning of the eighteenth century it belonged to the Duke of Grammont, then to the Duke of Orléans. It was transferred to England, and came into the Collections of Lord Berwick and Lord Darnley. In the Gardner Collection since 1896. It was begun in the summer of 1559 for Philip II, and, according to a letter dated April 26, 1562, was already sent to Spain that year.

Plate 89

PERSEUS AND ANDROMEDA. *Canvas, 179 × 197. London, Wallace Collection.* Formerly in the Collections of Philip II and then of the Dukes of La Vrillière and Orléans, of Sir G. Page Turner, and of the Marquess of Hertford. Titian promised this painting to Philip II in 1553, and it is mentioned by Dolce in 1557 as being among those the artist sent to Spain in 1557. Ricketts (1910) believes it to be a replica dating from about 1565 of the picture sent to Philip II. Tietze, on the other hand, identifies it with this actual picture, and dates it 1555. Pallucchini, who thinks on stylistic grounds that it was painted in 1562, puts forward the hypothesis that Dolce, seeing the picture just before it was finished, assumed that it was sent to Philip II later in 1557.

Plate 90

VENUS AND ADONIS. *Canvas, 107 × 135. Washington, D.C., National Gallery of Art, Widener Collection, 1942*. Came from the Barbarigo Giustiniani Collection in Padua, and was later in the Collections of Lord Bristol, of Lady Sutherland, and of the Earl of Spencer in London. Berenson believes it to be an authentic Titian; so does Tietze, who thinks it may be the model for the Prado painting (plate 57).

Plate 91

VENUS AND ADONIS. *Canvas, 122 × 135.5. New York, Metropolitan Museum*. Formerly in the Mariscotti Palace in Rome, then in the Collection of the Earl of Darnley, the Knoedler Collection, and the Bache Collection. It is another version of the Washington National Gallery of Art picture (plate 90). Berenson and Pallucchini, among others, believe it to be an authentic Titian; this latter critic dates it to after 1560. According to Tietze, on the other hand, it is a replica painted by Titian's workshop of the picture on the same subject in Washington, mentioned above.

Plate 92

PORTRAIT OF FABRIZIO SALVARESIO. *Canvas, 112 × 88. Vienna, Kunsthistorisches Museum*. Bears the date and inscription: MDLVIII. FABRICIUS SALVARESIUS ANNU AGENS L. TITIANI OPUS. Formerly in the Gallery of the Archduke Leopold William (1659, No. 32). See also plate 93.

Plate 93

PORTRAIT OF FABRIZIO SALVARESIO. Detail: the head.

Plate 94

PORTRAIT OF A MAN WITH FLUTE. *Canvas, 98 × 86. Detroit, Institute of Arts*. Signed: TITIANVS F. Formerly in the Von Stumm Collection in Berlin. Published by Hadeln (1926) as a late work. Tietze dates it about 1560; Pallucchini, probably later than 1561.

Plate 95

PORTRAIT OF A MAN. *Canvas, 87 × 70.5. Baltimore, Museum of Art, J. Epstein Collection*. Signed and dated: TITIANI OPVS MDLXI. Formerly in the following Collections: H. De Zoete; Pickhurst Mead, Hayes, England; C. Brinsley Marlay, Mullingar, Ireland. Art critics agree that this is an authentic Titian (Tatlock, 1925).

Plate 96

PORTRAIT OF A MAN WITH PALM. *Canvas, 138 × 118. Dresden, Gemäldegalerie*. Bears the inscription: MDLXI ANNO . . . NATUS AETATIS SUAE XLVI TITIANVS PICTOR ET AEQUES CAESARIS. Bought in Venice from the Marcello house before 1753. According to Cook (1904–05), Gronau, and Fogolari (1935), it represents Antonio Palma, nephew of Palma Vecchio and father of Palma Giovane. Tscheuchner considers it the portrait of an apothecary or doctor who had himself painted in the robes of a saint.

Plate 97

PORTRAIT OF LAVINIA. *Canvas, 103 × 86.5. Dresden, Gemäldegalerie*. Bears the inscription: LAVINIA TIT. V. F. AB EO F. Taken from Ferrara at the beginning of the seventeenth century to the Ducal Collection in Modena, and from here the Dresden Gallery acquired it in 1746. Tietze and Pallucchini date it to about 1565; Hadeln (1931) places it between 1555 and 1560, and believes that this is the picture which best lends itself to being identified as the portrait of Titian's daughter Lavinia.

Plate 98

SELF-PORTRAIT. *Canvas, 96 × 76. Berlin, Staatliche Museen.* Long ago, it was in the Barbarigo house at San Raffaele in Venice, then in the Solly Collection, and then purchased for Berlin in 1821. Gronau and A. Venturi date it 1550; Ricketts, 1558–60. Suida identifies it with the picture Vasari saw in Titian's studio in 1566 which had been painted four years earlier. Foscari (1935) accepts this hypothesis, and Pallucchini also accepts 1562 as the probable date of its execution.

Plate 99

MADONNA AND CHILD. *Canvas, 174 × 133. Munich, Bayerische Staatsgemäldesammlungen.* Signed: TITIANVS FECIT. Formerly in the Sacristy of the Escorial, where it is described by Francisco José de Siguenza in 1605. It belonged to General Sebastiani in 1810, and was bought from him in 1815 in Paris, and in 1836 was acquired by the Alte Pinakothek from the Hofgartengalerie in Munich. Morelli considered it to have been painted by Titian's workshop but completed by the master himself; however, contemporary art critics consider it to be an authentic late Titian. Tietze dates it 1560, Pallucchini proposes a dating around 1561 or slightly later, and suggests that this is the picture representing "Our Lady with the Child in her arms" which Titian told Philip II in April 1562 he was sending him together with *Christ in the Garden of Gethsemane* (plates 104 a and b) and *The Rape of Europa* (plate 88). According to Fischel, Titian had in mind a

Florentine model by Raphael when he was painting this picture. Siren (1902) lists a copy of the painting in the Aspelin Collection in Stockholm.

Plate 100

STIGMATIZATION OF ST FRANCIS. *Canvas, 295 × 178. Ascoli Piceno, Pinacoteca.* Signed: TITIANUS VECELLUS CADOR. Originally on the altar of the chapel of Desiderio Guidone, consecrated in 1561 in the Church of San Francesco in Ascoli. The picture may be dated a short time after the consecration of the altar. After its recent restoration (G. Urbani, 1951), Pallucchini quite rightly defined the collaboration of Titian's workshop to some of the less important sections of the painting. See also plate 101.

Plate 101

STIGMATIZATION OF ST FRANCIS. Detail: the head of St Francis.

Plate 102

THE DOGE ANTONIO GRIMANI BEFORE FAITH. *Canvas, 365 × 560. Venice, Ducal Palace.* This votive picture was commissioned from Titian by the Doge Francesco Venier on March 22, 1555. Begun as early as 1556, it was still unfinished when seen by Vasari in 1566. According to Suida and Tietze, the unfinished picture remained in Titian's workshop—thereby being saved from the 1577 fire—and was finished by Cesare Vecellio. Pallucchini also stresses the parts done by Titian's workshop.

Plate 103

THE TRANSFIGURATION. *Canvas, 245 × 295. Venice, Church of San Salvatore.* Mentioned by Vasari, who saw it in 1566 in Venice, it still overhangs the fourteenth-century silver *pala* of the main altar of San

Salvatore, although it has been repainted and is in a poor state of preservation. Fogolari (1935) and Tietze quite rightly date it about 1560.

Plate 104a

CHRIST IN THE GARDEN OF GETHSEMANE. *Canvas, 185 × 172. Escorial, Monastery of St Lawrence.* According to Cavalcaselle, it is the painting which arrived in Spain in 1562; Berenson, on the other hand, dates it before 1555, and Tietze between 1559 and 1562, considering much of it to have been painted by Titian's workshop. In any case, it is no longer possible to decide between this Escorial version and that in the Prado (plate 104b) which can be identified as the painting started in 1559 and sent to Philip II in 1562. Both canvases are mentioned in the 1574 inventory of the Escorial (Beroqui, 1946).

Plate 104b

CHRIST IN THE GARDEN OF GETHSEMANE. *Canvas, 136 × 176. Madrid, Prado.* (See note to plate 104a.) Cavalcaselle thinks that this painting is a poor forgery of Titian's style; Tietze believes it to have been painted by a Spanish imitator of the master—probably Francesco Navarrete, called Mudo. Berenson, however, considers it to be an authentic Titian painted after 1555, as does Pallucchini who stresses the new luminosity in its conception.

Plate 105

THE LAST SUPPER. *Canvas, 207 × 464. Escorial, Monastery of St Lawrence.* Begun in 1558, it was completed and sent to Philip II in 1564 (Cavalcaselle). No sooner had it arrived at the Escorial than it was cut at the top and sides to adapt it to the wall where it was to be displayed

(A. Alvarez Cabanas, 1934). According to Mayer (1938), the painting as it was originally is documented in a copy in the possession of the Earl of Ellesmere, while Tietze gives less credit to a sixteenth-century copy (170 × 216) in the Brera which is reproduced here. Tietze and many others think the Escorial picture was mostly painted by Titian's workshop; however, it has been damaged and repainted to such an extent that it is difficult to judge how much Titian's helpers painted.

Plate 106

PORTRAIT OF AN ORIENTAL POTENTATE. *Canvas, 158 × 112. Venice, Brass Collection.* Suida (1952) and Berenson (1957) have recently upheld the authenticity of this painting, and this attribution is borne out by the results of its recent restoration (1958). The identification with Selim II (1524–75) which Suida (1952) suggests is less likely. This critic dates the portrait to about 1571 by comparing it with the *Portrait of G. A. Doria* in the Contini Bonacossi Collection in Florence (see p. 95, Attributed Paintings), whose attribution to Titian, apart from anything else, is not very convincing.

Plate 107

ST NICHOLAS OF BARI. *Canvas, 171 × 91. Venice, Church of San Sebastiano.* Signed: TITIANVS P. Mentioned by Vasari in 1568, it was commissioned by Nicolò Crasso, the Venetian jurist, for the chapel he acquired in 1563 in the Church of San Sebastiano. Generally considered to be the work mainly of Titian's helpers—among them his son Orazio, according to Cavalcaselle and Pallucchini. Mayer (1938), dates it about 1540, Gronau between 1540 and 1550; however, there is no reason to doubt the fact that the picture was painted about 1563, the year in which Crasso acquired the chapel (Berenson, Tietze and Pallucchini).

Plate 108

THE ANNUNCIATION. *Canvas, 410 × 240. Venice, Church of San Salvatore.* Signed: TITIANVS FECIT FECIT. Mentioned by Vasari, and therefore painted before 1566. The dates 1560–66 suggested by Gronau have been narrowed to 1564–66 by Pallucchini. Tietze, who considers the second "FECIT" to be a restoration, believes there are traces of the date under this word. This does not seem to be so, however, on close direct examination. A preparatory study for the Angel of the Annunciation (drawing in charcoal pencil, 42 × 28) now in the Uffizi, is reproduced here. See also plate 109.

Plate 109

THE ANNUNCIATION. Detail: the head of the Angel of the Annunciation.

Plate 110

THE CRUCIFIXION. *Canvas, 216 × 111. Escorial, Monastery of St Lawrence.* Although it is not mentioned in the 1574 Escorial inventories, there is no doubt of its authenticity (Berenson, Suida, Pallucchini), and it was most probably painted about 1565 (Tietze).

Plate 111

THE CRUCIFIXION. Detail: the left-hand landscape.

LOCATION OF PAINTINGS

ANCONA

CHURCH OF SAN DOMENICO
*The Crucifixion, with the Virgin,
SS Dominic and John* (plate 74).

ASCOLI PICENO

PINACOTECA
Stigmatization of St Francis (plates
100 and 101).

BALTIMORE

MUSEUM OF ART
Portrait of a Man (plate 95).

BERLIN

STAATLICHE MUSEEN
*Venus, Cupid, an Organist and a
Little Dog* (plate 34).
Girl with Dish of Fruit (plate 63).
Self-Portrait (plate 98).

BESANÇON

MUSÉE DES BEAUX-ARTS
*Portrait of Nicolas Perrenot Gran-
vella* (plate 26).

BOSTON

ISABELLA STEWART GARDNER
MUSEUM
The Rape of Europa (plate 88).

CAMBRIDGE, ENGLAND

FITZWILLIAM MUSEUM
Venus and a Lute Player (plate 73).
Tarquin and Lucretia (plate 136).

CINCINNATI

MUSEUM OF ART
Portrait of Philip II (plate 42).

DETROIT

INSTITUTE OF ARTS
Portrait of a Man with Flute (plate
94).
Judith (plate 117).

DRESDEN

GEMÄLDEGALERIE
Portrait of a Girl (plate 61).
Portrait of a Man with Palm
(plate 96).
Portrait of Lavinia (plate 97).

EDINBURGH

NATIONAL GALLERY OF SCOT-
LAND
Diana and Actaeon (plate 84).
Diana and Callisto (plate 85).

ESCORIAL

MONASTERY OF ST LAWRENCE
St Margaret and the Dragon (plate
52).
St Jerome (plate 75).
The Adoration of the Magi (plate 76).
Christ in the Garden of Gethsemane
(plate 104a).
The Last Supper (plate 105).
The Crucifixion (plates 110 and
111).
The Martyrdom of St Lawrence
(plate 121).

FLORENCE

UFFIZI
Venus, Cupid and a Little Dog
(plate 35).
Portrait of Ludovico Beccadelli (plate
47a).

GENEVA

IN A PRIVATE COLLECTION
Portrait of Giovanni da Castaldo
(plate 28).

KANSAS CITY

GALLERY OF ART
Portrait of Antonio Perrenot Granvella (plate 27).

KASSEL

GEMÄLDEGALERIE
Portrait of a Gentleman (plates 40 and 41).

KROMIERIZ

NATIONAL GALLERY
The Punishment of Marsyas (plate 143).

LENINGRAD

HERMITAGE
Danaë (plate 59).
St Mary Magdalene (plate 112).
St Sebastian (plates 132 and 133).

LENTIAI (BELLUNO)

PARISH CHURCH
St Titian (plate 36).

LILLE

MUSÉE DES BEAUX-ARTS
The Stoning of St Stephen (plate 83).

LONDON

WALLACE COLLECTION
Perseus and Andromeda (plate 89).
NATIONAL GALLERY
Votive Portrait of the Vendramin Family (plates 14–19).
Venus and Adonis (plate 56).
Diana and Actaeon (plate 87)
on loan from the Earl of Harewood.
The Tribute Money (plate 126)
Madonna and Child (plate 139).

PRIVATE COLLECTION
Allegory of Prudence (plate 120).

LUGANO

THYSSEN COLLECTION
Portrait of Antonio Anselmi (plate 39).
Portrait of the Doge Francesco Venier (plates 50 and 51).

MADRID

PRADO
Ecce Homo (plate 20).
Portrait of Charles V at the Battle of Mühlberg (plates 22–24).
Portrait of Isabella of Portugal (plate 25).
Prometheus (plate 30).
Sisyphus (plate 31).
Venus, Cupid and an Organist (plate 32).
Venus and an Organist (plate 33).
Mater Dolorosa (plate 37).
Portrait of Philip II (plates 43, 44.)
Supposed Portrait of a Knight of Malta (plate 45).
The Adoration of the Holy Trinity (plate 53).
Bust of Christ (plate 54).
Mater Dolorosa (plate 55).
Venus and Adonis (plate 57).
Danaë (plate 58).
The Entombment (plate 79).
Salome (plate 82).
Christ in the Garden of Gethsemane (plate 104b).
St Margaret and the Dragon (plate 113).
The Entombment (plate 124).
Christ Carrying the Cross (plate 127).
Self-Portrait (plate 128).
The Fall of Man (plate 129).
Spain Coming to the Aid of Religion (plate 130).
Philip II Offering the Infante Don Fernando to Victory (plate 131).

MEDOLE (MANTUA)

CHURCH OF SANTA MARIA
The Risen Christ Appearing to His Mother (plate 64).

MELBOURNE

NATIONAL GALLERY OF VICTORIA
Portrait of a Franciscan Monk (plate 47b).

MILAN

AMBROSIANA
The Adoration of the Magi (plates 77 and 78).
BRERA
St Jerome in the Wilderness (plate 65).

MUNICH

BAYERISCHE STAATSGEMÄLDESAMMLUNGEN
Portrait of Charles V (plate 21).
Madonna and Child (plate 99).
The Crown of Thorns (plate 134).

NAPLES

CAPODIMONTE (NATIONAL GALLERY)
Pope Paul III and His Grandsons Alessandro and Ottavio Farnese (plate 1 and color plate I).
Pope Paul III Wearing the Papal Cap (plate 2).
Portrait of Cardinal Alessandro Farnese (plate 3).
Danaë (plates 4–5).
Portrait of a Girl (plate 6).
Portrait of Pier Luigi Farnese (plate 7).
Portrait of Cardinal Pietro Bembo (plate 10).
Portrait of Philip II (plate 48).

CHURCH OF SAN DOMENICO MAGGIORE
The Annunciation (plate 71).

NEW YORK

FRICK COLLECTION
Portrait of Pietro Aretino (plate 11).

METROPOLITAN MUSEUM
Venus and Adonis (plate 91).
Venus with the Lute Player (plate 72).

PIEVE DI CADORE

ARCHDIACONATE
Madonna and Child between SS Titian and Andrew (plate 125).

ROME

BORGHESE GALLERY
Venus Blindfolding Cupid (or *The Education of Cupid*) (plates 114–116).
St Dominic (plate 118).
Christ at the Column (plate 119).

ROTTERDAM

BOYMANS MUSEUM
Child with Dogs (plate 140).

ST LOUIS

ART MUSEUM
Ecce Homo (plate 135).

SAN FRANCISCO

DE YOUNG MEMORIAL MUSEUM
Portrait of a Friend of Titian (plate 46b).

SERRAVALLE (VENETO)

DUOMO
Madonna and Child in Glory, and SS Peter and Paul (plate 12).

STOCKHOLM

RASCH COLLECTION
Portrait of Philip II (plate 49).

VENICE

ACCADEMIA
The Deposition (plates 144–146).

BRASS COLLECTION
Portrait of an Oriental Potentate
(plate 106).

CHURCH OF THE JESUITS
The Martyrdom of St Lawrence
(plates 66–69).

CHURCH OF SAN LIO
St James of Compostella (plate 13).

CHURCH OF SAN SALVATORE
The Transfiguration (plate 103).
The Annunciation (plates 108 and 109).

CHURCH OF SAN SEBASTIANO
St Nicholas of Bari (plate 107).

CHURCH OF SANTA MARIA
DELLA SALUTE
Pentecost (plate 70).

DUCAL PALACE
The Doge Antonio Grimani Before Faith (plate 102).

SANSOVINIANA LIBRARY
Wisdom (plates 80 and 81).

VIENNA

AKADEMIE DER BILDENDEN
KUNST
Tarquin and Lucretia (plates 137 and 138).

KUNSTHISTORISCHES MUSEUM
Portrait of a Man with Book and Staff (plate 8).
Portrait of a Boy (plate 9).
Portrait of John Frederick of Saxony (plate 29).
Supposed Portrait of Benedetto Varchi (plate 38).
Danaë (plate 60).
Diana and Callisto (plate 86).
Portrait of Fabrizio Salvaresio (plates 92 and 93).
Portrait of Jacopo Strada (plates 122 and 123).
Nymph and Shepherd (plates 141 and 142).

WASHINGTON, D.C.

CORCORAN GALLERY OF ART
Portrait of Martino Pasqualigo (plate 46a).

NATIONAL GALLERY OF ART
Venus with a Mirror (plate 62).
Venus and Adonis (plate 90).

REPRODUCTIONS

ACKNOWLEDGMENT
FOR PLATES

Plates 1, 10, 20, 22, 25, 30, 31, 32, 33, 35, 37, 43, 44, 45, 47a, 48, 53, 55, 57, 58, 65, 70, 71, 74, 75, 77, 78, 79, 104a, 105, 110, 111, 113, 114, 115, 116, 118, 119, 127, 128, 129, 130, 131, 148b, 162b, 168, 179: *Anderson, Rome*. Plates 2, 96, 156a and b, 192; *Alinari, Florence*. Plates 3, 6, 7, 12, 38, 64, 72, 80, 81, 102, 103, 106, 107, 108, 112, 122, 123, 132, 133, 135, 149, 155a, 164b, 182: *Fiorentini, Venice*. Plates 13, 36, 66, 67, 68, 69, 125, 144, 159, 175: *Rossi, Venice*. Plates 100, 101: Istituto Centrale del Restauro, Rome. Plate 146: *A.F.I., Venice*. Plate 184: *Brogi, Florence*. Plate 185: *Gabinetto Fotografico Nazionale, Rome*. Plates 186a and b, 187a and b, 188, 189, 190, 191, 195, 197b, 198: reproduced from engravings. The remaining black and white plates were provided by the galleries and collections to which the pictures belong. Material for Color Plate I (Part 3) was supplied by Scala, Florence. Material for the other color plates in Parts 3 and 4 was supplied by the Prado Museum, Madrid.

PAUL III AND HIS GRANDSONS ALEXANDER AND
OTTAVIO FARNESE, Naples, Capodimonte

Plate 1. *Detail of color plate I*

Plate 2. PORTRAIT OF PAUL III WEARING THE PAPAL CAP
Naples, Capodimonte

Plate 3. PORTRAIT OF CARDINAL ALESSANDRO FARNESE
Naples, Capodimonte

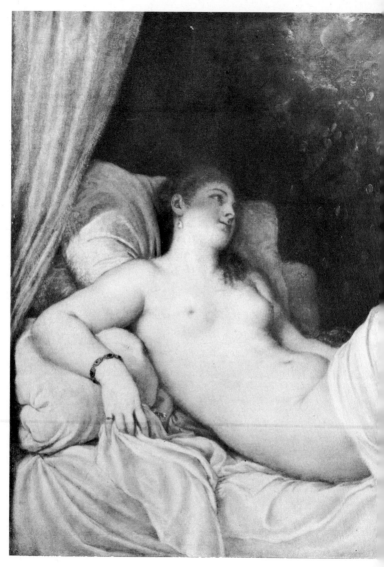

DANAË
odimonte

Plate 6. PORTRAIT OF A GIRL
Naples, Capodimonte

Plate 7. PORTRAIT OF PIER LUIGI FARNESE
Naples, Capodimonte

Plate 8. PORTRAIT OF A MAN WITH BOOK AND STAFF
Vienna, Kunsthistorisches Museum

PORTRAIT OF ISABELLA OF PORTUGAL, Prado, Madrid
(*detail of plate 25*)

Plate 9. PORTRAIT OF A BOY
Vienna, Kunsthistorisches Museum

Plate 10. PORTRAIT OF CARDINAL PIETRO BEMBO
Naples, Capodimonte

Plate II. PORTRAIT OF PIETRO ARETINO
New York, Frick Collection

Plate 12. MADONNA AND CHILD IN GLORY, AND SS PETER AND PAUL
Serravalle, Duomo

Plate 13. ST JAMES OF COMPOSTELLA
Venice, Church of San Lio

Plate 14. VOTIVE PORTRAIT OF THE VENDRAMIN FAMILY
London, National Gallery

Plate 15. *Detail of plate 14*

Plate 16. *Detail of plate 14*

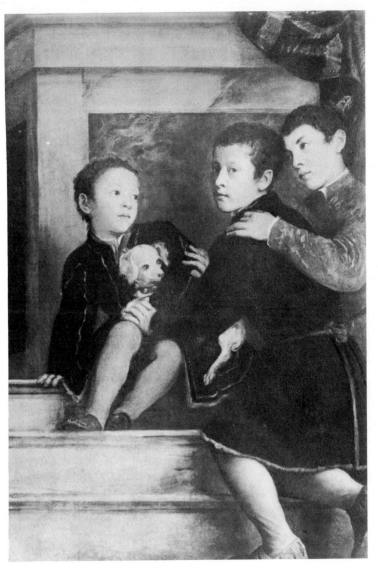

Plate 17. *Detail of plate 14*

Plate 18. *Detail of plate 14*

Plate 19. *Detail of plate 14*

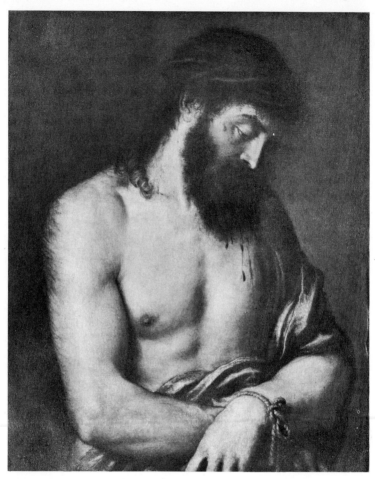

Plate 20. ECCE HOMO
Madrid, Prado

Plate 21. PORTRAIT OF CHARLES V
Munich, Bayerische Staatsgemäldesammlungen

Plate 22. PORTRAIT OF CHARLES V AT THE BATTLE OF MÜHLBERG
Madrid, Prado

Plate 23. *Detail of plate 22*

Plate 24. *Detail of plate 22*

Plate 25. PORTRAIT OF ISABELLA OF PORTUGAL
Madrid, Prado

Plate 26. PORTRAIT OF NICOLAS PERRENOT GRANVELLA
Besançon, Musée des Beaux-Arts

Plate 27. PORTRAIT OF ANTONIO PERRENOT GRANVELLA
Kansas City (Missouri), Gallery of Art

Plate 28. PORTRAIT OF GIOVANNI DA CASTALDO
Geneva, private collection

Plate 29. PORTRAIT OF JOHN FREDERICK OF SAXONY
Vienna, Kunsthistorisches Museum

Plate 30. PROMETHEUS
Madrid, Prado

Plate 31. SISYPHUS
Madrid, Prado

Plate 32. VENUS, CUPID AND AN ORGANIST
Madrid, Prado

Plate 33. VENUS AND AN ORGANIST
Madrid, Prado

Plate 34. VENUS, CUPID, AN ORGANIST AND A LITTLE DOG
Berlin, Staatliche Museen

Plate 35. VENUS, CUPID AND A LITTLE DOG
Florence, Uffizi

Plate 36. ST TITIAN
Lentiai (Belluno), Parish Church

Plate 37. MATER DOLOROSA
Madrid, Prado

Plate 38. SUPPOSED PORTRAIT OF BENEDETTO VARCHI
Vienna, Kunsthistorisches Museum

Plate 39. PORTRAIT OF ANTONIO ANSELMI
Lugano, Thyssen Collection

Plate 40. PORTRAIT OF A GENTLEMAN
Kassel, Gemäldegalerie

PORTRAIT OF PHILIP II, Madrid, Prado
(*detail of plate 43*)

Plate 41. *Detail of plate 40*

Plate 42. PORTRAIT OF PHILIP II
Cincinnati, Museum of Art

Plate 43. PORTRAIT OF PHILIP II
Madrid, Prado

Plate 44. *Detail of plate 43*

Plate 45. SUPPOSED PORTRAIT OF A KNIGHT OF MALTA
Madrid, Prado

Plate 46. PORTRAIT OF MARTINO PASQUALIGO
Washington, D.C., Corcoran Gallery of Art
and

PORTRAIT OF A FRIEND OF TITIAN
San Francisco, De Young Memorial Museum

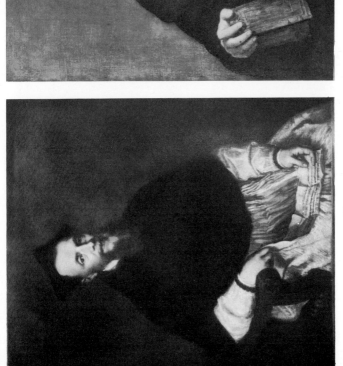

Plate 47. PORTRAIT OF LUDOVICO BECCADELLI
Florence, Uffizi
and

PORTRAIT OF A FRANCISCAN MONK
Melbourne, National Gallery of Victoria

Plate 48. PORTRAIT OF PHILIP II
Naples, Capodimonte

DANAE, Madrid, Prado
(*detail of plate 58*)

Plate 49. PORTRAIT OF PHILIP II
Stockholm, Rasch Collection

Plate 50. PORTRAIT OF THE DOGE FRANCESCO VENIER
Lugano, Thyssen Collection

Plate 51. *Detail of plate 50*

Plate 52. ST MARGARET AND THE DRAGON
Escorial, Monastery of St Lawrence

Plate 53. THE ADORATION OF THE HOLY TRINITY
Madrid, Prado

Plate 54. BUST OF CHRIST
Madrid, Prado

Plate 55. MATER DOLOROSA
Madrid, Prado

Plate 56. VENUS AND ADONIS
London, National Gallery

Plate 57. VENUS AND ADONIS
Madrid, Prado

Plate 58. DANAË
Madrid, Prado

Plate 59. DANAË
Leningrad, Hermitage

Plate 60. DANAË
Vienna, Kunsthistorisches Museum

·Plate 61. PORTRAIT OF A GIRL
Dresden, Gemäldegalerie

Plate 62. VENUS WITH THE MIRROR
Washington, National Gallery of Art

Plate 63. GIRL WITH DISH OF FRUIT
Berlin, Staatliche Museen

Plate 64. THE RISEN CHRIST APPEARING TO HIS MOTHER
Medole (Mantua), Church of Santa Maria

Plate 65. ST JEROME IN THE WILDERNESS
Milan, Brera

Plate 66. THE MARTYRDOM OF ST LAWRENCE
Venice, Church of the Jesuits

Plate 67. *Detail of plate 66*

Plate 68. *Detail of plate 66*

Plate 69. *Detail of plate 66*

Plate 70. PENTECOST
Venice, Church of Santa Maria della Salute

Plate 71. THE ANNUNCIATION
Naples, Church of San Domenico Maggiore

Plate 72. VENUS WITH THE LUTE PLAYER
New York, Metropolitan Museum

Plate 73. VENUS AND A LUTE PLAYER
Cambridge, Fitzwilliam Museum

Plate 74. THE CRUCIFIXION, WITH THE VIRGIN, SS DOMINIC AND
JOHN
Ancona, Church of San Domenico

Plate 75. ST JEROME
Escorial, Monastery of St Lawrence

Plate 76. THE ADORATION OF THE MAGI
Escorial, Monastery of St Lawrence

Plate 77. THE ADORATION OF THE MAGI
Milan, Ambrosiana

Plate 78. *Detail of plate 77*

Plate 79. THE ENTOMBMENT
Madrid, Prado

Plate 86. WISDOM
Venice, Sansoviniana Library

Plate 81. *Detail of plate 80*

Plate 82. SALOME
Madrid, Prado

Plate 83. THE STONING OF ST STEPHEN
Lille, Musée des Beaux-Arts

Plate 84. DIANA AND ACTAEON
Edinburgh, National Gallery of Scotland

Plate 85. DIANA AND CALLISTO
Edinburgh, National Gallery of Scotland

Plate 86. DIANA AND CALLISTO
Vienna, Kunsthistorisches Museum

Plate 87. DIANA AND ACTAEON
London, Earl of Harewood, on loan to the National Gallery

Plate 88. THE RAPE OF EUROPA
Boston, Isabella Stewart Gardner Museum

Plate 89. PERSEUS AND ANDROMEDA
London, Wallace Collection

Plate 90. VENUS AND ADONIS
Washington, National Gallery of Art

Plate 91. VENUS AND ADONIS
New York, Metropolitan Museum

Plate 92. PORTRAIT OF FABRIZIO SALVARESIO
Vienna, Kunsthistorisches Museum

Plate 93. *Detail of plate 92*

Plate 94. PORTRAIT OF A MAN WITH FLUTE
Detroit, Institute of Arts

Plate 95. PORTRAIT OF A MAN
Baltimore, Museum of Art

Plate 96. PORTRAIT OF A MAN WITH PALM
Dresden, Gemäldegalerie

Plate 97. PORTRAIT OF LAVINIA
Dresden, Gemäldegalerie

Plate 98. SELF-PORTRAIT
Berlin, Staatliche Museen

Plate 99. MADONNA AND CHILD
Munich, Bayerische Staatsgemäldesammlungen

Plate 100. STIGMATIZATION OF ST FRANCIS
Ascoli Piceno, Pinacoteca

Plate 101. *Detail of plate 100*

Plate 102. THE DOGE ANTONIO GRIMANI BEFORE FAITH
Venice, Ducal Palace

Plate 103. THE TRANSFIGURATION
Venice, Church of San Salvatore

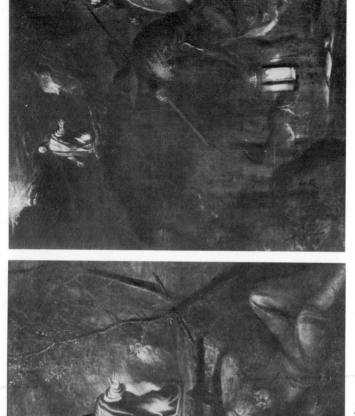

Plate 104. CHRIST IN THE GARDEN OF GETHSEMANE
Escorial, Monastery of St Lawrence, *and* Madrid, Prado

Plate 105. THE LAST SUPPER
Escorial, Monastery of St Lawrence

Plate 106. PORTRAIT OF AN ORIENTAL POTENTATE
Venice, Brass Collection

Plate 107. ST NICHOLAS OF BARI
Venice, Church of San Sebastiano

Plate 108. THE ANNUNCIATION
Venice, Church of San Salvatore

Plate 109. *Detail of plate 108*

Plate 110. THE CRUCIFIXION
Escorial, Monastery of St Lawrence

Plate 111. *Detail of plate 110*